**This book is to be returned on or before
the last date stamped below.**

Circus !

Circus!

An Investigation into what makes the sawdust fly

BY

Alan Wykes

London
Jupiter Books (London), Ltd.
1977

First published in 1977 by
JUPITER BOOKS(LONDON) LIMITED
167 Hermitage Road, London N4.

Copyright © Jupiter Books (London) Limited 1977.

ISBN 0 904041 77 8

Composed in 12pt Monotype Bembo, Series 270,
and printed and bound in Great Britain by
R. J. Acford Limited, Chichester, Sussex.

Contents

Urchin with pipe and tabor, performing
bear, and monkey. Engraving by Thomas
Bewick (1753-1828).

Introduction

I CAN'T CLAIM THAT THIS BOOK WILL DO YOU ANY GOOD AT ALL – MORAL, physical or financial. It won't tell you how to become a funambulist, a lion-tamer, or a bearded lady; it won't enable you to levitate, equestriate, prestidigitate, or juggle. And if I say it won't you can take it from me it won't; because I wrote it. Neither will it tell you how to start a circus; still less will it provide the money to do so. On the other hand, since it is the highly idiosyncratic book of an idiosyncratic writer who relishes poking about on the fringes of things, you may well find odds and ends and anecdotes that even if you're an *aficionado* of circuses and fairgrounds you may not have come across before. The Big Top, for instance. Do you know how it came into being? The revelation may astonish you. (On the other hand, of course, it may not.) Madame Zazel – who was she? Have you come across her in any other book about circuses and fairs? Well, you may have, but it doesn't matter; even if you have you almost certainly don't know what happened to her. I do. And I tell all, nothing suppressed.

You will probably know something of the history of circuses and fairs already (if you don't you're going to get double value for your money), and another claim I can't make is to have discovered anything fresh in the historical field. There was never much doubt about the chronological road along which the showman trundled; and it would have been more than idiosyncratic – in fact, it would have been less than sensible – to force it into some procrustean frame for the sake of novelty. So you'll find the beginning of the tale somewhere near the front of the book and the end at the back – though despite the difficulties encountered by Count Lazard (there's another unfamiliar name referred to herein), the death knell hasn't tolled for the circus yet.

Another thing: virtually every book about circuses I've come across, and every personal narrative I've listened to, has been in some way concerned with the training of performing animals and the risks attendant thereto. But not this book, not this personal narrative. I've explained why in my book; but another reason is that it's pointless to duplicate what has been done so elaborately before. Explanation and repetition also account for my not having gone to town, as the phrase has it, on clowns – which, however amazing it may seem, I am not over-enthusiastic about.

What, then, is left? I will tell you. What you have here is a record of a search into the byways, nooks, and crannies of circus history. My method has been to avoid repeating what is widely known, for instance, 'General' Tom Thumb and the Siamese Twins – famous examples of Barnum's penchant for physical curiosities – and to mention instead such improbable circus acts as Brigham Young the Mormon and his many wives, and Grace Darling, the heroine of the *Forfarshire* rescue. Who would have thought? But it's true.

Well, I did say it was an idiosyncratic book. You have been warned. But if you've got this far, read on. The gallimaufry that lies before you may not cover virgin ground, but it reaches into some barely trodden corners.

Circus!

Coloured cut-outs of circus characters
were popular children's toys in
the nineteenth century.

1.

The Roar of the Greasepaint

THE NOTICE SAID 'ENTER THROUGH THE CAMELS.' I COULDN'T UNDERSTAND IT.
Camels passing through the eyes of needles I knew about; but people passing
through camels was a completely new idea. I asked my mother. She replied
distractedly, 'It's just a way of saying it's the way in, over there, where the camels
are.'

'But,' I persisted with incipient pedantry, 'you don't go through the camels, you
go through the place where they are.'

'Much more of that sort of talk,' she said, 'and we don't go at all.'

Thus threatened I kept my counsel.

The pay box was indeed between two enclosures in each of which were three of
these oddly constructed beasts. I didn't know then that some sardonic soul had
described the camel as 'a horse put together by a committee'. I didn't know then
that it is a creature of great character: supercilious, smelly, spiteful if unnerved (it
kicks viciously), and liable to reward anyone it doesn't particularly care for by
farting or spitting. Either way the smell is disgusting; and if you happen to be
drenched in its spit your company will be unendurable to any other human being
for at least three weeks. The camel has considerable dignity, however, particularly
in its sexual habits. Both males and females come into season, the males exhibiting
their state by foaming at the mouth and nose and discharging purulent matter from
an excrescence on the forehead. Very unpleasant. But their satisfaction is obtained
in a most orderly way. The female stands rear-end-on to her beaux, who form a
file like a bus queue. Number one in the file then mounts, achieves his orgasm,
dismounts, and returns to the end of the queue, while the next one takes his turn,
and so on. This goes on until honour and everything else is satisfied – probably a

'If you don't stop fidgeting I'll
put you down.' Blondin, the
famous rope-walker.

couple of hours. An exemplary procedure. I wish I'd known about it that day in 1922 when I was taken to the circus for the first time; I would have looked at the camels with higher regard. As it was I looked at them with scorn. I thought they were merely misshapen and unlikely to perform any interesting tricks. (I was right there: they don't. But ridden in the ring by veiled and voluminously robed girls, walking with dignified measure to the sound of vaguely 'Persian Market' music, they do add a touch of the mysterious East.) My concern that day was not really for animals at all. Trapeze artists, high-wire walkers, jugglers, and acrobats were what I had come for. My father as a young man had seen Blondin walking a wire stretched between the two towers of the Crystal Palace, and the very thought of this remarkable equilibrist excited me. He'd been dead for twenty-five years at the time of my visit, but the excitement he generated had infected me. Besides, he made me laugh. My father had quoted the memorable admonition Blondin had made to the man he was carrying on his back across Niagara Falls: 'If you don't stop fidgeting I'll put you down.' Even at the age of eight, I thought that a good joke. One way and another I had the feeling that the circus would provide me with a much-needed boost to my morale, which was low at the time on account of various domestic tribulations – including a punitive reduction of pocket money – resulting from what my mother called my 'acting up'. Acting up was any activity that reaped parental wrath; and I had scraped into the long-promised circus visit only on condition that acting up would not be included in my curriculum for an unspecified future period. Hence my concern to keep my counsel over the matter of entering through the camels.

I may say that the circus fulfilled my every expectation. 'The roar of the grease-paint, the smell of the crowd', as some joker has transposed it, had entered into my soul. So boring did I become in rehashing the entire performance for the second-hand entertainment of any captive audience that chanced into my company, that telling about the circus edged into acting up. 'That's enough now,' my mother admonished as I once again began to recall the miracle of the trapezists' double backward somersault. 'You're acting up.' After that I kept my recollections to myself – but so besotted was I with them that I became a collector of circus *memorabilia*. My bedroom walls became plastered with prints of old posters,

Jean Polaski, a trick equestrian in
the ring at Astley's Circus.

handbills, throwaways, press cuttings, admission tickets, coloured reproductions of Big Top paintings, sepia vignettes of Barnum and Lloyd and Hengler and Sanger stiffly posing in Victorian photographers' studios against backgrounds of potted palms and marble pillars, advertisements cut from provincial newspapers announcing the arrival of the Greatest Show on Earth in the readers' midst next Saturday, with the Big Parade ('Fully authorized by the local constabulary') starting its journey at midday and blazing its way through the town ('The Bandsmen in Full Uniform') to arrive at the venue where 'The World's Finest and Largest Circus Tent' would be erected in time for the first performance at 6 p.m. As young people nowadays surround themselves with pictures of pop stars, so I gazed upon engravings of Mazeppa's Ride, Ducrow's dancing horse Pegasus, and Astley's Amphitheatre of the Arts. I fingered through portfolios of cheap prints in Leather Lane and in courts off Charing Cross Road, and bought anything that was within my means and had a circus flavour, however grubby or tattered it might be. (Successful erasing of dirty marks could often be accomplished with breadcrumbs, and transparent music tape repaired frayed edges.) I was the circus buff of Wallington, Surrey. True, few people beat a path to my door in search of knowledge; but I took pride in the fact that had they done so I could have given them a rundown on practically anything that had ever happened within the purlieus of the Big Top. I had a vague idea of starting up a Circus Information Bureau, convincing myself in the dreamy way of children (or anyway the sort of child I was) that all that was needed was an advertisement in the paper, which would settle me for life with an ever-increasing income from the millions clamouring to know Blondin's real name (Jean François Gravelet), the salary paid to the first human cannon-ball (£120 a week), the functions in acrobatics of understanders, middlemen, and top mounters, and similar bits of arcana. There were, in fact, no clamouring millions (and no advertisement, come to that); and a year or two later circuses were replaced in my affections by the films – the transition having been made with perfect smoothness by my being taken to the cinema to see *He Who Gets Slapped*, an adaptation of Andreyev's play about a disenchanted intellectual who seeks refuge from the uncomprehending world by becoming a circus clown. Off with the circus, on with the flicks.

Tutored animals.

Then, in 1930, when I was caught, like everyone else, in the midst of one of the numerous links in the chain of disasters (euphemistically known as depressions) that statesmen shackle us with, I read in *The Times* (the issue of 11 November) that 'Processions are good things, and there is never a better time for the circuses than when the bread is dear or scarce'. Juvenal had said something akin to that nearly two thousand years earlier in his *Satires* ('Two things only they earnestly desire, bread and the games of the circus'); but I hadn't then read Juvenal, and anyway *The Times* was nearer my condition at the time, for I had but half-a-crown to my name (twelve and a half pence in the plastic confetti now called money). I could have done with a procession to take the edge off the thought of my penury – for there's not much doubt about it, the sound of trumpets and drums and the colour and excitement of the parade through the streets as a prelude to the performance is a pleasing distraction to those keeping warm in the public library and rattling the coppers in their pockets as they wait for something to turn up.

What turned up in my case was an invitation from a neighbouring family, the Inghams, to accompany them as their guest on a visit to Mitcham Fair.

The Inghams were relatively well off: they owned both a motor car and a Philips wireless set that was powered not by accumulator and high-tension batteries but by the electricity supply – a wondrous novelty in those days. This evidence of affluence was not accompanied by any evidence of upstart superiority. The Inghams were *plebs* like the rest of us in the road (which was called, rather grandly, South Avenue), and they put on no side. Their daughter Marjorie was a childhood sweetheart of mine. We had been to the same kindergarten school and had shared a desk, giggled over hidden copies of *Tiger Tim's Weekly*, and drooled over bars of Sharp's Kreemy Toffee; and on one occasion I'd pulled her out of the pond in the local park, into which she'd tumbled in an excess of enthusiasm to capture a minnow. Her parents thought they owed me a debt of gratitude for saving her life, which in truth was hardly in danger, since the pond was barely two feet deep. But I'd remained the blue-eyed boy and they never missed an opportunity of giving me what they called 'little treats'. This particular little treat included travelling with Marjorie in the dicky of the Swift coupé, hands on each other's knees, eyes reflecting each other's adoration, all the way to Mitcham – a matter of

Putting up tents for a circus, 1886.

three miles or so. Bliss! As we bumpety-bumped along the side roads by which we approached Mitcham Common (it was only long afterwards that I realized Mr Ingham's discretion in keeping off the thoroughfares where the disapproving glares of passers-by might have inhibited our adoration) I wished the journey would never end. But as someone sings in *Rigoletto*, 'La donna è mobile'; and not only is woman fickle, man is too. Both of us ran dry of romantic endeavour as, faintly at first then ever louder, we heard the splendid sound of the fairground calliope – a thing of beauty mundanely defined by the dictionary as 'a series of steam whistles played from a keyboard like an organ'.

Immediately I was back at the entrance through the camels of eight years earlier. My suspended loyalty re-sensitized, I felt the same anticipatory excitement. You may reasonably argue that my excitement was misplaced, that fairs and circuses are not the same, which up to a point is true. But together with pantomimes and music hall entertainments they are reflections of similar urges in mankind to entertain and be entertained, to attempt (and sometimes achieve) the impossible, to sing and make merry because tomorrow we pass on (and anyway, there isn't all that much difference, as I shall demonstrate in the pages to come). The point is, that revived that day by the steam-whistled sound of 'Ramona', the cries of the barkers calling all within earshot to enter and observe the charms of the hairy lady or whack the weight up the scale to hammer the bell, the screams of the girls on the Big Dipper as their skirts blew up over their heads, and the giants and pygmies and mermaids and elastic-skinned men ('I will guarantee to you, ladies and gennelmen, that 'e will wrap 'is own 'ead in folds of skin from 'is chest, and your money back if 'e don't'), and other unfortunates mocked by nature – revived by these my enthusiasm entered a new phase. The circus *memorabilia* had long vanished from my walls and been replaced by stills from *Metropolis*, *The Singing Fool*, *The Cabinet of Doctor Caligari*, and similar classics of my second love; and I had even in my kinematic enthusiasm made acquaintance with a projectionist, Ernie Healing by name, who on scheduled evenings projected films in the local village hall and had immense difficulty in synchronizing the dialogue, which was recorded separately on discs, with the movements of the actors' mouths – a difficulty that caused much merriment. But now, as I heard the quack medicos taking advantage of the transient

A horse beating a tabor, from
a medieval woodcut.

location of the fairground to unload their panaceas upon a gape-mouthed peasantry, I felt myself once again entranced by the roar of the greasepaint, the smell of the crowd, and submitted, like Pinocchio, to the garishness, noise, and promise of fantastic marvels to be seen. I banished the flicks to a much smaller pigeon-hole in my department of enthusiasms and opened up the floor space to, as it were, 'The Entry of the Gladiators' – the spell of the clowns.

A clown from a French illustrated circus book.

2.

Bring on the Clowns . . .

ANCIENT ROME IS AS FAR BACK AS WE NEED TO GO IN TRACING THE HISTORY OF the circus; though as with many other manifestations of man's determination to be up and doing, scrapping, showing off, and in general expressing himself, we could go further – to man's beginning, in fact. But we'll settle for Rome in the years before Christ, space for recording footprints in the sands of time being a bit cramped.

The Roman festivals in the early days, when Rome was no more than a junior republic, combined business and pleasure: they were meant to placate the malign forces of nature (which could ruin the crops if you didn't coddle them with sacrificial blood) and at the same time give people an opportunity of venting their emotions. In time the sacrificial element became symbolic rather than real, but the number of festivals grew until, by the fourth century A.D., so many births, accessions, consecrations, and the like had been made the excuse for celebration that virtually half the year – 177 days, to be exact – was given over to holidays; which was one reason why the Roman Empire declined and fell. But the manner rather than the number of festivals is my concern here.

A *spectaculum* was any large enclosure (the word 'amphitheatre' came later) in which the goings-on were held, and it wasn't necessarily circular, though the two principal *spectacula* of Rome were called the Circus Flaminius and the Circus Maximus; more often it was elliptical or oval. The Emperor Augustus elaborated the simple stone and timber structure with its rising tiers of seats by adding twelve starting boxes for the magistrates who presided and signalled the opening of gladiatorial contests and chariot races; he also added exterior arcades where there were shops, restaurants, sideshows, and free trafficking in the services of prostitutes

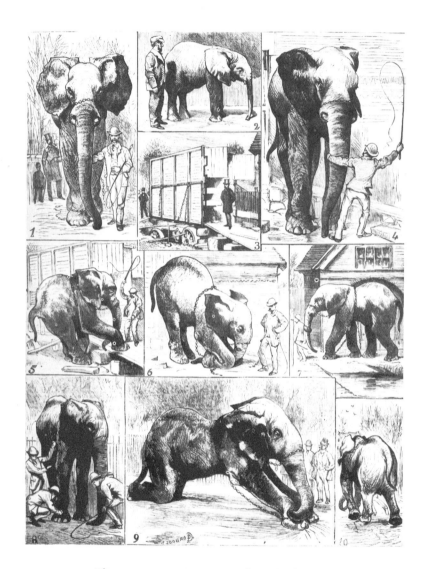

The attempt to remove Barnum's Jumbo from the
Zoological Gardens, 1882.

and astrologers. Already, as you see, there appears a basic similarity to the modern fairground with its inducements to wallow in the smaller fleshpots. But if the origins of Mitcham Fair can be seen in Augustan Rome, so can the predecessors of Barnum & Bailey, Sanger, Bostock, the Ringling Brothers, Bertram Mills, Chipperfield, Billy Smart, *et alii* be traced to the impresarios of the days of the Caesars. Most of them came from Egypt and were supposed to have mystic powers over animals. The probability is that they had only what all animal trainers must have: patience and understanding. At all events, they provided us with the first noteworthy performing domestic and wild animals – performing, that is, in an arena for the entertainment of the paying public.

Horses were for the most part used for chariot racing, though there were some displays of equestrian skill involving trick riding, standing on the chariot-pole or on the horses' backs, or somersaulting on the yoke; but the wild animals – elephants, lions, crocodiles, hippopotamuses, tigers sent from India, seals, ostriches, and many other exotic creatures – were taught tricks and displayed in cages as novelties. The tricks were very similar to those performed in the circus today. Plutarch tells of a dog that simulated death by poison, exhibiting hideous convulsions first, then, when his cue was given, rising to his feet and frisking about. There were monkeys costumed as soldiers driving teams of goats harnessed to chariots; elephants that sat at a dining table and consumed food with the utmost refinement, turning to each other the while and nodding as if in conversation; elephants walking the tightrope; bears shinning up poles and afterwards collecting contributions from the audience in silver bowls; lions that jumped through hoops; polar bears sporting with seals in pools contained in marble baths. On one occasion there was a near-disaster when at the festival planned by Pompey in 55 B.C. he had eighteen elephants brought from Africa on the promise that after they had entertained the crowd in the Circus Maximus they would be returned to their native land. Betrayal replaced the promise. The emperor ordered that the beasts should be fought by javelineers. Thus goaded, Pliny tells us, 'the elephants stampeded and made for the iron railing between the arena and the spectators; they raised their trunks and screamed, as if imploring mercy. Among the spectators terror for their own safety combined with pity, and they shook their fists angrily at

An eighteenth-century print showing deadly
combat between gladiators and wild
animals in the *spectaculum*.

Pompey. Was there not some affinity between man and this clever, noble beast? Had the elephants not been promised, and in their intelligent way understood, that their lives would be spared and that they would be returned in safety?' Pompey got his just deserts, the Romans said, when he was assassinated in Egypt in 48 B.C.: it was the elephants' revenge. All the same, spectators at subsequent displays in which elephants took part were protected by a moat between them and the arena.

Besides the performing animals, acrobats, equilibrists, jugglers, and equestrians, there was another marked similarity between the Roman circus and ours. The stone seats can hardly have been comfortable, but a much greater source of discomfort was the heat of the sun in summer, which had to be endured for many hours, for no member of the populace was allowed to leave while emperor, senators, or magistrates remained in their sun-shaded boxes. Julius Caesar considerately ordered that an immense awning should be made to cover the *spectaculum*. It was supported by ships' masts and hauled up with tackle operated by sailors. This original version of the Big Top was extremely troublesome in high winds, which caused it to crack and flap and sometimes tear; but it also provided a beautiful effect of light, for the canvas awning was assembled from many different-coloured sections and the result was a gorgeous dappling of red and yellow and purple on the arena below. 'All within', the poet Lucretius wrote, 'laughs in the flood of beauty, when the light of day is thus confined'.

Regrettably, there was carnage as well as floods of beauty. The populace whose sense of fair play surfaced when Pompey's elephants were treacherously treated could as easily enjoy the spectacle of armed men fighting, or hunting animals, in the *spectaculum*; animals of different kinds – lions and bulls, for instance – pitted against each other; and convicted criminals thrown unarmed to numerous beasts that had been smoked out of their cages and driven with goads into the arena. Cicero attacked the sadism of such entertainments: 'How can there be any pleasure for a civilized being in the mangling of a weak man by a powerful beast, or the transfixing of a splendid beast by a hunting-spear?' How, indeed? But the acclamation of the crowd was proof. 'The frenzied shrieks demean man to a level lower than that of animals in the wildness of their native place; for there at least the strongest must slaughter the weakest to ensure survival.'

Jesters dancing, from a thirteenth-century manuscript.
Popular entertainments soon found expression
in early art forms.

Survival in the Roman form was not part of the circus's lot. The decline of an empire sees the rise of an austerity that cannot be accommodated within the leisure arts, no matter what Juvenal and *The Times* may say. As that diligent historian Gibbon tells us: 'The value of any object that supplies the wants and pleasures of mankind is compounded of its substance and form, of the materials and the manufacture. Its price must depend on the numbers of persons by whom it may be acquired and used; on the extent of the market; and consequently on the ease or difficulty of remote exportation, according to the nature of the commodity, its local situation, and the temporary circumstances of the world.' The circumstances that deprived the Romans of their holidays were temporary indeed: an infinitesimal scrap out of the ragbag of time. Rome was sacked by Goths and Vandals, Christians and Barbarians; and in a few brief centuries Europe was reconstructed along different lines. But whatever the guidelines within which man operates, his personal pleasures are never far from the centre of his consideration. Having satiated those aspects of his nature dedicated to greed and brutality, he turns to less laborious forms of pleasure, among which has always been that of watching other people work – particularly if the form of activity is one in which the beholder sees himself, with a little effort, emulating the beheld, or one in which he is flattered and cajoled into casting aside the small garment of critical judgement and assuming in its place the voluminous mantle of willing self-deception. Thus it is always pleasurable to watch contests in which victory for one of the combatants is the end product, and equally pleasurable to become a willing advocate of a worthless panacea, gape at the unusual and manifestly impossible, and adopt the conviction that one can outwit the superior skill of the trickster. Into one of those categories virtually everything that could be witnessed in the Circus Maximus and similar *spectacula* could be grouped: gladiatorial engagements and the remarkable results of animal training to be seen in the arena itself; quack physicians, astrologers, freaks, jugglers, acrobats, illusionists, and anticipatory versions of the three-card trick (done with three walnut shells and one small pebble), to be found in the arcade side-shows. And when the tumult and the shouting of Gothic and Vandal conquest had died down the colossally expensive and elaborate apparatus of the Roman circus had been replaced by the tournament and the travelling show of the Middle Ages.

Tumbling, thirteenth and
fourteenth centuries.

The origins of the tournament are obscure. It may have developed from the equestrian games of the German tribes, though the first recorded tournaments date from the tenth century. The Roman *spectaculum*, like the modern circus, was an entertainment mounted by professionals as an exotic change from everyday life. The tournament, on the other hand, grew out of everyday life, as practice for warfare, and became a sport in which armed knights on horseback displayed their martial prowess in mock combat. The emphasis was always on participation – for both fame and profit. People of all classes attended tournaments, but only knights could take part, and by the fourteenth century tourneys were becoming the exclusive preserve of wealthy nobles, who alone could afford the increasingly elaborate and expensive plate armour.

The lower orders concentrated instead on another, equally robust, branch of entertainment. In effect, they separated the venues of the public entertainment and the semi-private one. Clutching, so to speak, at the adjunctive arcade that had titillated the curiosity and minor lusts of those Romans who for one reason or another were opting out of a particular display in the *spectaculum*, they adopted it as their own and moved it around like a pedlar with a pack on his back. In that way the travelling show came into being; and once in being it proved to be as worthy of elaboration as any other idea that catches on.

The travelling show always attached itself, necessarily if parasitically, to an existing institution: the medieval fair (derived from *feriae*, the clerical Latin word for holidays), a large annual market that was sensibly held on the day of a saint's feast to ensure that as many people as possible were available for trading. Since the fair and its traders and customers were already, so to speak, a captive audience, it was equally sensible for peripatetic entertainers and hangers-on to silt up where the best business might be found. They were well aware that whoever gets the best of a bargain – and for that matter whoever gets the worst of it – is likely to be in a mood to be entertained and to distribute rewarding largesse. The impresarios among them took their freaks and exotic animals, the jugglers and conjurers and equilibrists and acrobats their apparatus, the quacks and abortionists and astrologers and pimps the testimonials to their immaculate honesty and the quality of their products (or, in the case of the abortionists, their non-products) from the pens of the

Making the poker hot in a country
theatre.

mighty or from bribed witnesses who accompanied them and could be relied on to convince the illiterate peasantry. Eventually they were joined by strolling players and musicians who also had offerings to put before any good-humoured crowd, and, more important, by specialists in the arousing of laughter. About these specialists, the clowns, a word must be said, for they became in time the indispensable adjunct of all circuses; but with, at the outset, a declaration: I have never been specially amused by circus clowns in general (and with circus clowns I include those who have branched off slightly on to the stage – for example, Grimaldi and Grock, of whom more in a moment). Their grotesqueries and drolleries leave me for the most part unmoved. Their repetitive jokes and activities with buckets of whitewash seem to me too often laboured and drawn out. If there is amusement to be gained from the throwing of one custard pie – which there may be, though not, for me, in very high degree – there is not automatically double, triple, and quadruple amusement to be gained from the throwing of two, three, or four custard pies. The somewhat reluctant twitch that with me passes for a smile when the first custard pie follows its parabola and lands on the face of the fall guy is the beginning and end of the joke so far as I am concerned. This, I realize as the tumult of laughter surrounding me increases with each new besmirching of the loon's features, is my loss and the gain of countless others. However, the promised word:

Joseph Grimaldi is said by many to be the archetypal clown. Mistakenly, in my view. Grimaldi, whose parentage is uncertain, though his mother was said to be a Mrs Brooker, was a Londoner born in 1778. He went on the stage as a child and developed into an extremely versatile actor who could play comedy, tragedy, and farce equally successfully. He appeared as a comic 'in drag', but because of the wide range of his voice could also movingly portray parts normally given to tragediennes. He could convincingly be the cat in *Dick Whittington*, a drunkard, a cannibal, an evil spirit, a king, a glutton, a monster, a dancer, or an acrobat. He made people laugh, but he could also make them cry, which is not one of the objects of clowning. So surely he was a wide-range actor rather than simply a clown; but it is as a clown that Grimaldi's name has come down to us, and not as the teacher of the actor Edmund Kean (which he was), as a skilled magician (which he also was), or as one who could play Richard III with hair-raising effect. All clowns have

Balancing a chair and diving
through a barrel of fire;
a French engraving of the
eighteenth century.

since been called Joey after him; and, partly because he was such a master of disguise and appeared – it was said – 'in a thousand different faces', they have adopted the practice of creating, each for himself, an individual makeup and character as different from every other clown's as is one fingerprint from another. No clown would dream of imitating the clothes or particular grotesquerie of another clown; such plagiarism would only earn him the condemnation of the entire profession. The variations, as I say, are endless; but basically there are only two types of clown: the red-nosed and the white-suited. When in partnership it is the red-nosed one who does all the spraying of water, the sloshing about of white-wash, and the chucking of custard pies, and the white-suited (and invariably white-faced) one with his pom-poms and conical hat who is at the receiving end of all the slapstick. The innocence of white and the rumbustiousness of red emphasize the symbolism, the eternal conflict between he who does the slapping and he who gets slapped. Solo clowns combine the two elements of the conflict within one personality. And such a one was Grock.

Grock was his clown's name, Adrien Wettach his real one. He was Swiss, born in 1880, and for a year or two toured continental music halls with a partner called Brick in an act mingling acrobatics, ballet, and knockabout comedy. His solo act, which was immensely popular in London and Paris, was lost to England when he was hounded from the country in 1924 by the impossible demands made by the Inland Revenue. The situation was typical of the one he exploited in his act: he was always the underdog jauntily fighting back at life's intolerable ironies. (Grock and Chaplin have the same basic humour, but to me Chaplin's is infinitely more subtle.) He was a pianist whose stool was permanently too far from the keyboard but who ingeniously coped by moving the piano nearer to the stool; he was a violinist continually perplexed by the right way of holding the instrument; he continually sympathized with himself in his distress and warmly appreciated his own felicitous jokes; he challenged gravity by putting his fiddle on the sloping lid of the piano and bidding it stay there, and gleefully discovered that he could stop its downward progress by holding it there with his grotesquely big-booted foot. Over everything except the Inland Revenue he triumphed; and he wanted others to share his joy. To make certain that they did there was a lot of repetition which I

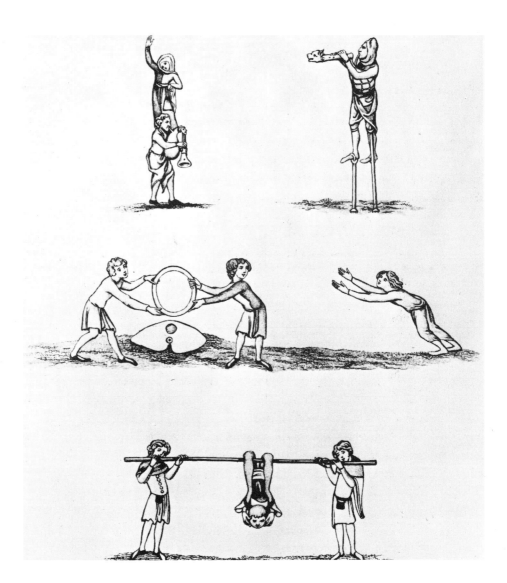

Town life in the Middle Ages; illustrations
from a fourteenth-century manuscript.

and the likes of me found too protracted. The goings-on could be seen through like
a tunnel with a light at the end of it. So alas no: the generally accepted version of
the clown – famously typified by Grimaldi and Grock – is not for me. (There is,
nowadays, a tendency to include within the classification such geniuses as Chaplin,
the Goons, the Marx Brothers, and similar artistes; and about them and their like I
hold different views because my reaction to them is to be reduced to helpless
laughter. But this is a book about circuses, not about the vaudevillians of stage and
screen.) However, if despite my declared insensitivity I may have your attention, I
will outline something of the historical path of 'clods, clots, lumps'. Bring on the
clowns.

*   *   *

Buffoonery – to use a less clumsy word than 'clownery' – is older than the sportive
games of the *spectaculum*. Jokes as such, and jokers to make them, are not recorded
on the frescoes of ancient Egypt, but there's an Egyptian hieroglyph to describe a
mask – the disguise affected by one who wishes to pretend to be another character,
in short an actor. In the theatre of Attic Greece the players were too far from the
spectators to express emotion through the features. As with clowns' makeup,
exaggeration was necessary. A mask with thick upturned lips and another with the
lips pursed and drooping could unmistakably signal comedy and tragedy, however
great the distance. Colour helped: purple and blue and white for the draperies of
those portraying the heavies; red and yellow or quarterings of several colours for
those engaged in light relief or comedy. The symbolism persists to this day, as may
be seen in any representation of a court jester's costume, which, with its Punchinello cap and bells, is an instant symbol for laughter. Motley and the mask, like
the red nose and the white suit, have become immediately recognizable as
simulations of all emotions needed to fit the story-line. From ancient Egypt to
modern television comedy the game of Let's Pretend has involved disguise and the
substitution of one personality for another. 'The frolick of the clowne and the
teares of the tragedious personne', says a fifteenth-century plug for the theatre,
with unwitting profundity, 'takyth a manne from himself.'

The first clown was a 'clod', a clodhopper, a witless oaf who in time learned

A 'Joey', in traditional make-up inspired by
Grimaldi.

cunning as we have seen but who at first was pitiful and in a sense miraculous, for the derangement of his mind was a visitation from God. His antics, like those of the Fool in the Morris Dance, had a lunatic logic of their own that could not be shared by more rational – allegedly more rational – people, who were awestruck by the uncomfortable thought that perhaps the pitiful clod was the only one in step with life. An astute onlooker observing the antics of a fool and the sympathy he gained had not far to go to the comprehension of imitation. In Athens, C. M. Bowra tells us, there was a clever pauper who tired of his poverty and turned it to riches by acting foolishly before the crowds entering the theatre. This first recorded busker, whose name was Selin, wore trousers, a garment not then fashionable and never previously seen in Athens. This and his carefully assumed vapid expression convinced the arriving audience that Selin was a messenger of the gods and that they had better distribute alms to be on the safe side. Otherwise plans might go awry and the Eumenides come knocking at the windows. But they were rewarded for their largesse otherwise than with the smug satisfaction of placating the gods: Selin spun about in comical attitudes, fell down foolishly, pretended to be a child crawling and a dog barking, and smothered his face with a muddy concoction he carried in a jar at his waist, and in general clowned about in much the same way that today's circus clowns perpetrate their grotesqueries. He became something of a public figure and it was not long before a new form of comedy – burlesque – sprang into being, with broad comedians who owed much to Selin's acts and contrivances. But although the first nameless clodhopper had unwittingly established the basis for the art of clowning, and Selin had cunningly wormed his way into the act for his own advantage and turned witlessness into wit and profit, and thereby opened the gates to a professional coterie that so far as one can tell will be with us till the sawdust runs out, there is a long gap in the roll-call of names. Three centuries pass before we find another named clown, one Stratocles, in the records of Quintilian, who in his twelve-volume treatise on public speaking, gives high praise to this *stupidus* of the Roman theatre. (The *stupidus* was the generic clown of those days. His head was always shaved, he wore a gross phallus, and carried a stick for laying about with. Centuries later the *Commedia dell'arte* would produce clownish variations in Harlequin, Pantaloon, Fool, and Punchinello; but the basic

A woodcut of the sixteenth century
showing tumblers jumping
through raised hoops.

type remained the *stupidus*.) Stratocles came to an untimely end on his birthday. Having given a great performance he followed it with a dinner party at the end of which he called for a warm drink, set his phallus and thrashing-stick on the table before him, and lay back and relaxed. When the assembled company pointed out that his drink was getting cold the words failed to arouse him. He was dead.

Not so, however, his art. Clowns continued to flourish, brandishing their slapsticks, phalluses, and other appurtenances, through the period of rule and misrule that followed the Roman Empire. They sank somewhat from public view and instead became something of a cult among the élite, the lordlings and pseudo-monarchs whose burdens of rapine and conquest made them melancholy, or who had been defeated and needed the consolation of laughter even more urgently. Excepting the nomadic barbarian Huns who, as Ammianus Marcellinus pointed out, were singularly ill-humoured ('beasts on two feet, small, squat, hideous, who neither cook nor season their food and lifelong are riveted to their horses, where they eat, drink and sleep, bent over the lean necks of their mounts holding counsel'), the oligarchs of the Dark Ages were not short on the capacity to laugh. The grimly named Vandal king Godigisel (fifth century A.D.) died in battle but died laughing, having heard a last merry quip spoken by his fool, a Roman slave called Saunio. Thorismund the Goth, during his reign of two years (451–3), collected into his court a number of entertainers all of whom he called Euric in memory of his homosexual lover, who had (so it says in Schmidt's *Die Ostgermanen*) 'delighted him day and night with grimaces and tumbles'. And Charles Martel, who drove the Moors from France at the battle of Poitiers in 732 (with, it is said, the aid of the newly discovered equestrian accoutrement the spur), was as licentious a king as ever was and between battles dedicated to the spreading of the Christian doctrine loved nothing better than to hold court and entertain his guests with feasting and the performances of minstrels and tumblers, and particularly to summon before them 'his clown Terence who from birth had been afflicted with a humped back and hideous features but had acquired the habit of making mock of himself in such subtle ways that he caused all about him to laugh merrily'.

During the years between the Dark Ages and the Renaissance, when (not to shirk a cliché) Europe was in the melting pot, clownship became a respected –

Tutored bears.

indeed an enviable – profession because of its association with the top echelons of society. But battles and their consequences sprawled across the Continent – and indeed beyond into Africa and the East – in such riotous profusion that there was little time or chance for plebians to entertain or be entertained. In the Far East the market and the caravanserai had their quota of tale-tellers and dancers, but strolling players had not yet strolled upon the scene, and amid holocausts and slaughter would not have been likely to receive a very warm welcome anyway; so public entertainment takes a deep dip in the affairs of nations until the higher cultures of medieval Europe swept over the devastation and re-established an aesthetic anchorage. The form it took, so far as public entertainment was concerned, was that of the travelling show that attached itself to the market-place. And there we may now look not only for clowns but also for the beginnings of the circus as we know it today.

*   *   *

In the early Middle Ages, itinerant entertainers of all kinds – minstrels, tumblers, jugglers, clowns – found their audiences chiefly in the castles and manor houses around which the feudal system revolved. With the growth of the towns, however, the travelling show was more profitably established in the market-place, and here it quickly became evident that there was no limit to the novelties the audience was prepared to accept: stilt walkers elevated as high as a house; sinuous snakes coiled in baskets from which their wicked heads could be charmed by players on pipes; musicians who simultaneously conjured noises from drum and tabor and lute; conjurers who pulled impossible measures of brightly coloured silk from the gaping mouths of collaborators from the crowd; gymnasts who twisted themselves into impossible shapes and poses; clowns who enacted amusing obscenities and did not even draw the line at the occasional blasphemy; lumbering bears shackled by iron gyves and rattling their chains as they lugubriously danced; splendid white horses pawing the air as the little dogs mounted on their backs jerked at the reins; and the high- and slack-wire walkers as they trod their narrow course between the two towers of the scaffolding they erected themselves. Nor was there any limit to the noise and confusion that resulted from rival showmen trying to capture the attention of an audience. Tempers ran high and podia erected to elevate the showmen above

A performing horse and its trainer,
with spectators behind
wooden barriers.

the heads of the crowd were brought low in scuffles to gain the earliest attention of those watching for amusement. Confusion became worse confounded if those whose impresarios were clamouring for spectators were wrestlers and they decided to take sides in a dispute; injury and even death were not unusual when such a fracas broke out, and pickpockets had a royal time dipping into the purses of those whose attention was distracted. The upshot of such violence, which over the years gradually increased much as violence at football matches has increased today, was that different showmen tended to withdraw from the immediate vicinity of the market-place and to erect portable booths or small theatres on the outskirts of the village or town. These gave a double advantage: the freaks and performers and animals were not in direct open competition with each other; and the showmen, by enticing the public to pay an admission fee, did not have to rely on voluntary contributions that depended on the whim of the audience and were directly related to individual enjoyment. But 'pay first, see the marvels afterwards' had its disadvantages too. It depended on the power of enticement. Gradually the show-man or his appointed agent perfected a technique of sales talk that was difficult to resist. Curiosity being instinctive in human beings, and exaggeration being one way of arousing it, the crier or bellman (not until the end of the seventeenth century was the name 'barker' bestowed upon him) developed a good line in hyperbole. By the sixteenth century all abnormally oversized people were 'giants' or 'the greatest creature ever set before human eyes'; horses with false horns fixed to their foreheads were 'unicornes with the power of inducing potency by the mere touch of their mystic member'; animals came 'from the plaines of Cathay' or from 'Libya's mighty mountains'; misshapen dwarfs had their origin 'where the Kingdome of Hungary meets the Danube'; magicians were Eastern and had powers 'inherited from the tombes of Egypt'; acrobats were 'nature's wonders born without bones'; and for everything this was the first, last, and only time of showing – if no move was made immediately in the direction of the booth 'but a field away beyond the brook' then a lifetime would have been wasted and for all his ensuing years the non-beholder would rue the day. People were just as credulous then as they are today, and the rasping but honeyed tongues of the criers lured them quite easily. In any case, though there were naturally shysters among the

A roughly executed woodcut depicting a
rope-walker at Bartholomew Fair.

tempters, there *were* wonders to be seen, and as Phineas T. Barnum, the biggest shyster of them all, was to discover centuries later, it is conviction that counts, not truth: if people are convinced that what they are looking at is a pig with two heads, then a pig with two heads it is.

All this vulgar shouting, however, was no attraction in the homes of the upper crust, and became even less so as strangely exotic monsters such as crocodiles and rhinoceroses were added to the attractions and equestrian acts demanded more and more space. Knights and their ladies had tolerated – indeed enjoyed – the parlour entertainments of juggling, tumbling, and jesting, but hairy men and bearded ladies, limbless dwarfs and alarming crocodiles, were considered distasteful and not at all the sort of thing for a gentleman's residence. So gradually the second of the two venues where the itinerant showman might find a customer for his wares disappeared from the realm of the possible. (The rich, like the poor, are always with us and can have what they want when they want it; and it is true that throughout the ages there have been those whose tastes run to fairs and circuses and who have had such enterprises brought into their very front gardens. Charlemagne was one, Mahmoud of Gahzni was another, William Beckford when living in Switzerland was another, William Randolph Hearst another; and only the other day, in November 1976, the Sultan of Oman air-lifted an entire circus from Enfield, Middlesex, at a cost of £150,000, so that he could watch it at home on his birthday.) But it was really of little moment that the private customers were fading away. Country fairs were growing in popularity, and although in Chaucer's day there were still possible engagements in the courts and castles of the high-born, it was on the village green or in the fields surrounding townships that menageries, freaks, puppets, clowns, performing animals, and performing people were to be found on Fair days. Also to be found was a great deal of coarse bawdiness which is brilliantly reported in Ben Jonson's *Bartholomew Fayre*, the tale of Bartholomew Cokes, simpleton, his servant Waspe, Mr Justice Overdo, and the Puritan do-gooder Zeal-of-the-land Busy, most of whom end up in the stocks being humiliated in consequence of mistaken identities, while all around them showmen and their criers call the crowd to attention with all the enthusiasm of a muezzin summoning the faithful to prayer.

A rope-walker ascending St Mark's Tower at Venice,
from an anonymous Italian woodcut of
the sixteenth century.

Jonson's play was produced in 1614. Nearly a century earlier Archbishop
Cranmer had expressed his vexation at the riotousness with which fairs were
conducted on holy days: 'In our time, God is more offended than pleased, more
dishonoured than honoured upon saints' days, because of pride, drunkenness,
idleness, quarrelling, brawling, and the watching of strange doings in the booths of
the unrighteous given in public upon the sward near the church or in the fields near
to the graveyard. There may be seen fairs and markets, wakes, ales, May-games,
rush-bearings, bear-baites, dove-ales, bonfires, and all manner of unlawful gaming,
piping, dancing and suchlike; with the ungodly who shriek "Rar-ee-show!" and
summon the people from mass to the plenitudes of sin.' But his protestations were
to no avail. The merchants who sold their cloth at the fairs held in London, Bath,
Bristol, Oxford, and Winchester had a powerful hold on the nation's commerce,
and the stage had now been reached where the sideshows attracted people to their
displays and increased their business rather than the reverse. 'At one time,' wrote
Faux, the famous fifteenth-century illusionist, 'it was the devil and alls task to make
haste to the cloth fair or the cheese fair before all custom had vanished before us;
but now it is the merchants who seek us out and beg us to attend that they may do
lively busyness; for folk will walk out of theyre way to see a three-breasted
woman or a learned pig and may thereby be trapped into buying cheese or ginger-
bread or jewjaws for their finery.' Faux modestly refrained from mentioning that
he was one of the greatest attractions at any big fair. Belatedly, in 1731, the
Gentleman's Magazine described one of his illusions: 'He raised up before the very
eyes of those aghast at it, an apple tree which bore ripe apples in less than a minute,
and several of the crowd present tasted thereof and went away wondering. Indeed
a farmer who was of the company offered to pay Monsieur Faux a great sum if he
would but come to his orchard and make a similar tree to grow there, so that they
might share in the profit of selling the fruit. But Faux refused, saying it was but a
trick he was performing and that it was for the merriment of the spectators only
and not for the confusion of the general populace. At which the farmer went away
marvelling.' As well he might.

You will have noted that on to the entire corpus of fairs and the performers
therein there had rubbed off a patina of roguery – immorality, if you like. It was

Tricks taught to horses are shown in these illustrations
collected from medieval manuscripts.

frowned on not only by top clerics like Cranmer but also by those who were, or thought themselves to be, mere gentlefolk. Sons were warned, daughters were forbidden, fairs were put out of bounds. The fable of the Grasshopper and the Ant, the tale of Pinocchio, and moralities of soberer stuff were brought to bear as the Puritan hangover that persisted after the Restoration made a desperate effort to stifle everybody with its fumes. But it was a thankless task for the thunderers of doom. Gentlefolk might fuss and bother, but *hoi polloi* outnumbered them four to one and anyway were entitled to their pleasures, coarse though they might be. The shambles and immoralities of the fair tightened their grasp. They rivalled the theatres – not only in supposed immorality and wickedness but in trade too, so that in the summer months, when the fairs and pleasure gardens had the advantage of providing outdoor amusement, the theatres were forced to close and give best to the

> *Shrill fiddling, sharp fighting, and shouting and shrieking;*
> *Fifes, trumpets, drums, bagpipes, and barrowgirls squeaking*

of the fair. But the theatres had the last laugh – or perhaps one should say the penultimate laugh, for a seventeenth-century ordinance by the Grand Jury of Middlesex designating fairs 'a public nuisance, harmful to the peoples' and forbidding their engagement on any public ground scarcely had the power of its convictions, and after a short space of time local authorities were empowered to make their own regulations with regard to the visitations of amusements ('Fully authorized by the local constabulary').

You will have observed that thus far, though we have the component parts of the circus – the Big Top itself in an early form, the equestrian feats in the form of Roman riding, the clowns and freaks and acrobats and trained animals, the jugglers and equilibrists – they have not yet been assembled as a whole. How they came to be so assembled, on sawdust, and girt about by a ring, is a matter for the next chapter.

A woodcut from an early-
nineteenth-century
playbill.

3.

...and the Horses...

NEVER MIND WHAT THE MANCUNIANS SAY: THERE ARE SOME THINGS THAT London thinks of first. One of them was the idea of an establishment for the teaching of *haute école*, the advanced forms of horsemanship. The idea was not, of course, new even to London, for the Spanish Riding School in Vienna had been established in the sixteenth century, and there were others on the Continent with similar objects. There were already places in England where young ladies and gentlemen were taught the arts and graces of riding, but the idea as dreamed up – separately – by Jacob Bates, Thomas Price, and William Sampson, all residents of villages round London (Islington, Highgate, and Mile End), in the early years of the eighteenth century, was not for a school for teaching the rich but rather for an exhibition of trick riding that would make the populace marvel and after- wards become pupils – on the principle of the beholder seeing himself, with a little effort, emulating the beheld.

Jacob Bates had been a famous riding-master in France, but the economic depres- sion following the War of the Spanish Succession had obliged him to return to England, where he attached himself to a band of travelling showmen. His talents as a rider capable of remarkable feats of horsemanship were quickly recognized and he attracted great crowds at the country fairs he attended. Sensibly, he saw little future in making money for others and quickly broke away to start on his own, establishing himself first at Lincoln's Inn Fields, where the legal fraternity found much in his exhibitions to amuse them during adjournments of the courts. He presently teamed up with one Johnson, an Irishman, and word of mouth publicized their feats so quickly that soon Lincoln's Inn wasn't big enough to accommodate the crowds – which in any case were disturbing the tranquillity of

A dancing bear. Pen and ink drawing by
H. Bunbury (1750–1811).

the place – and they sought fresh fields and a new clientele at Harrow-on-the-Hill, some miles to the north and too far from London for an unhorsed population to trudge: an advantage quickly seized by Bates' rival Thomas Price, who put the following advertisement in the *Courier*:

> Mr Price will exhibit Horsemanship, this and every afternoon if the Weather Permits, in a field adjoining to The Three Hats at Islington: Where Gentlemen and Ladies may be accommodated with Coffee and Tea, Hot Loaves, and Sullybubs, the Loaves to be ready at Half an Hour after Four O'Clock every afternoon, by your humble servant, Joseph Dingley.

This Dingley was the landlord of the Three Hats and in his association with Price acted in the office of impresario. Clearly he had a good eye for business – the refreshments are evidence of that. Bates, Price, and Dingley had hit upon an idea that stirred the public interest at precisely the time it was ready to be stirred. Its readiness was brought about in large measure by the inability of the theatre to provide popular entertainment. Congreve, Wycherley, and the other Restoration playwrights offered witty, subtle comedies that mirrored the libertine notions of the aristocracy but had no common touch about them. Soon the upper crust were the only people who went to see them. The lower crust sought for something that would later be provided by that monument to boredom, poet laureate, and playwright of the unactable and unreadable, William Whitehead, in *The School for Lovers* and similar models of purity and high-flown sentiment. (Odd, perhaps, for people who during the entire period of the Commonwealth had had no theatre to go to; but then no one has ever denied that people are odd.) Meanwhile the lacuna in the provision of popular entertainment was filled with immense success by exhibitions of horsemanship. No one had seen such amazing tricks before: standing in the saddle, turning a somersault thereon, dismounting and remounting in an instant while the horse was at full gallop, turning round in the saddle and directing the horse by signals on its flanks – there seemed to be no end to the skill displayed. Price flourished; likewise Dingley. Then one day another advertisement appeared in the *Courier*:

> Mr Price begs leave to return his sincere and hearty thanks to those Ladies and Gentlemen who have been so kind in honouring him with their Appearance at Islington, and hopes to

A modern circus woodcut maintains the
great tradition of circus
graphic art.

deserve a continuance of their Favours; but Tomorrow he is engaged (by Desire) to ride at a particular Place for that Day only.

It was the beginning of the end. 'Desire' was only too proper a word to describe his entanglement with a woman. She had approached him by letter – a letter in which she asked if Mr Price would consider giving her lessons in the Noble Art of Riding, of which she knew nothing but was willing to learn. His suspicion that she meant a different sort of riding from that of horsemanship was confirmed. He became absolutely besotted with her, and she with him. His equestrian skill, understandably, suffered. Once or twice his tricks were mistimed and he nearly came a cropper. He needed more and more time off to recover from his excesses. Disappointed audiences booed when he boobed, demanded their money back when he failed to appear. Dingley warned him twice, then dissolved the partnership. He had read in the *Courier* that 'Mr William Sampson, lately discharged from Lord Ancram's Light Dragoons' gave displays at the Weaver's Arms, Mile End, for which members of the audience were willing to pay one shilling each for admission – threepence more than Price had rated. Dingley made his way to Mile End, saw, and was conquered by the Light Dragoon's skill. He took him into partnership immediately and with a buildup worthy of an advertising campaign mounted by J. Walter Thompson launched him on the tumultuous sea of an audience who by now knew their stuff and were prepared to criticize as well as applaud. They found everything to applaud and little to complain about in Sampson's horsemanship; he could ride not only one horse but two simultaneously, a booted and spurred foot placed on the bare back of each; he could jump them both over a four-foot fence as he stood upon their backs and fired two pistols into the air; he could roll himself sideways under the belly of his mount and rise up on the other side like the sail of a windmill revolving while going at full gallop; he could stand on his hands on the saddle, moving his legs in the air like scissors, very droll. Edward, Duke of York, honoured the Three Hats with his presence not long before he died in 1767, and sent his A.D.C. to Sampson with a message of congratulation in which His Royal Highness was quoted as saying that 'he had not seen the like before'.

This increasingly marvellous series of performances not unnaturally created a

Astley's riding school near Westminster Bridge.

demand for even more daring and fantastic feats. Rivals to Dingley's enterprise sprang up everywhere. A horseman named Daniel Wildman gave a performance involving bees, the like of which had never been seen either. While standing upright he conjured his swarm of bees to settle on his head and face, then fired a pistol to command them to part into two swarms, settle in formation on two tables, and return to their hive at the signal from a second pistol shot. He was taken to the hearts of the public much as a pop singer is taken today, and could go nowhere without being lionized in the homes of his rich and poor adorers. (One family who had scraped up the entrance fee to see his performance offered him their youngest nubile daughter for a night if he would but raise their standing among their neighbours by arriving at their door on his well-publicized mare, Merryfoot. Unfortunately it is not recorded whether or not he accepted this offer of pleasurable comfort.)

Very soon the fit-up drama companies that went the rounds of the fairs found it necessary to ensure that there were equestrian turns either on the stage or nearby so that they could be certain of their audiences. 'The rage', wrote Horace Walpole, 'is for horses, horses, horses, and for riders who are not mere riders but who can train the animals and perform upon them as if their very lives depended upon it' – which, of course, they did. In retrospect it can be seen very clearly (a particular characteristic of retrospect, it always seems to me) that there could not have been a better time or a better social background in which and against which to establish the circus. There was dire poverty, politics and justice were rife with corruption, hospitals demanded £1 burial fee before they would admit you as a patient (you got it back if you recovered – or anyway that was the theory), England was hardly in a rosy situation internationally, and, except for the wealthy, times were as they so often are – hard.

*　　　　　*　　　　　*

In November 1759, Philip Astley, a seventeen-year-old apprentice cabinet-maker, left his home in Newcastle under Lyme after a furious row with his father over the precedence in Philip's life of horses over cabinets. He tramped to Coventry,

Rope-walkers on the high-rope are suspended from poles
braced by many supports in this seventeenth-century
German engraving.

where the annual horse fair was going on, and there, through cold, swirling fog, glimpsed a performance by what the *Daily Courant* called 'The Famous Company of Rope-Dancers Unparallized'. The seventeenth-century diarist John Evelyn had gone overboard about an earlier company of rope-dancers, of whom the most famous was called 'The Turk':

> I saw even to astonishment the agility with which he performed. He walked barefooted, taking hold by his toes only of a rope almost perpendicular, and without so much as touching it with his hands. He danced blindfold on the high rope, and with a boy of twelve years old tied to one of his feet about twenty feet beneath him, dangling as he danced, yet he moved as nimbly as if it had been but a feather. Lastly, he stood on his head, on the top of a very high mast, danced on a small rope that was very slack, and finally flew down the perpendicular, on his breast, his head foremost, his legs and arms extended, with divers other activities.

The *Courant* was able to multiply the wonders:

> At the Great Booth over against the *Hospital* Gate, will be seen the Famous Company of Rope-Dancers, they being the greatest performers of Men, Women and Children that can be found beyond the Seas, so that the World cannot parallize them for dancing on the Low-Rope, Vaulting on the High-Rope, and for walking on the slack, and Sloping Ropes, out-doing all others to that Degree, that it has highly recommended them, both in *Bartholomew* Fair and *May* Fair last, to all the best persons of Quality in *England*. And by all are owned to be the only amazing Wonders of the World, in every thing they do: 'tis there you will see the *Italian* Scarramouch dancing on the Rope, with a Wheel-Barrow before him, with two Children and a Dog in it, and with a Duck on his Head. The whole Entertainment extremely fine and Diverting, as never was done by any but this Company alone.

Astley was diverted all right; but although the marvels of the Famous Company registered in his mind there was an even more diverting diversion round the corner from the Hospital Gate: there, smart N.C.O.s of King George's army were conducting a recruiting campaign: 'Here's Colonel Eliott, aide-de-camp to his Majesty, come here to enlist you in his new regiment, the Fifteenth Dragoons. Let powdered hair, drums and colours, speak for themselves; and if you have a mind to whet your whistles with His Majesty's double beer, follow me.'

At the end of that journey was the uniform of Eliott's Light Horse, the 15th

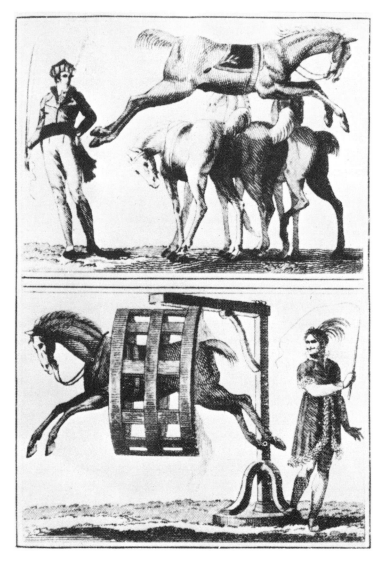

Two finely engraved hand-coloured plates from
a French circus history.

Dragoons, and the famous action against the French at Emsdorf and Warburg, where the Duke of Brunswick was killed and Astley covered himself in glory when he seized an enemy standard from the very heart of a mêlée and later presented it to the king. In seven years he rose from private to sergeant-major and then bought his discharge for the sum of one shilling – his 'service to king and country and general proper demeanour' having entitled him to a virtually free discharge. He then made his way to London.

Astley's voice was in the tradition that has been followed in recent years by the stentorian Regimental Sergeant-Major Brittain of the Grenadier Guards. His word of command, his commanding officer said in his discharge papers, could be 'clearly heard and understood at a distance of greater than one mile.' (Doubtful, one would have thought; but *The Guinness Book of Records* had not then begun its presentation of astonishing facts, so nothing was lost.) Not only was his voice tremendous in decibels, however; he also was 'a horse breaker and trainer of great skill, to whom all things come easily in the manner of wresting from the beast all that is best in it. With men he is firm and commanding and will give them no quarter in idleness.' One can imagine him on the parade ground, bellowing at some hapless rookie, 'You thar, you idle man! Move yourself! Or h'are you to stand thar all day as if the 'airs of your h'arse was tied together?' Even less printable things can be imagined if my own experiences with sergeant-majors are anything to go by (which they are – but not, alas, in this book). I need not disappoint you, however, concerning Sergeant-Major Astley's perspicacity in summing up the situation affecting public entertainment. His beady eye saw the possibilities immediately. By the grace of the gods that dispense the fortune that arranges for people to live at the right time for their particular talents he leapt into the fray with all the enthusiasm he had shown at Emsdorf, reinforcing it by marrying first a thoroughgoing horsewoman whom he called, with an unexpected disregard for the booming protocol of the army, Petsy. He then went off to Smithfield Market and bought a pair of horses, choosing carefully and reporting to Petsy, 'This 'ere h'animal has eyes bright, lively, resolute, and h'impudent that will look at a h'object with a kind of disdain; and this other h'animal, though not so bright of h'eye, 'as a willing tendency to be taught tricks such as Zucker's

The strong men.

Learned Little 'Orse has done to tremendous h'acclamation at Belvidere Gardens h'up there at Pentonville. They will be a worthy h'acquisition, the pair of 'em.' Which, indeed, they were, particularly the impudent one that was easy on the learning, and on the word of command (which must have frightened the very wits out of him if Astley used his voice at full volume) pawed the name Astley letter by letter in the sawdust, distinguished between gold and silver, could count up to twenty, would delicately extract a handkerchief from the pocket of a lady or gentleman, and would sham dead when told to fight for the Spaniards (he became renowned as 'the Spanish Horse'). In addition to these two horses Astley had a white charger that his commanding officer had presented him with on giving him his discharge from the army, and this charger he would ride, wearing the full rig of the Dragoons, round and round a field called Halfpenny Hatch, in the corner of Lambeth Marsh. Having attracted attention he would hand out bills to the crowd advising them to come that very afternoon and enjoy, for sixpence, 'the greatest wonders of the world, offered in all humility at four in the afternoon on Saturdays and Sundays only until Demand makes further performances the Vital Necessity'.

'The greatest wonders of the world' were well received, the hyperbole presumably being ignored as it is today when found on detergent packets and the like, for Astley had some remarkably good turns. He had remembered the success of the rope-dancers at Coventry and had secured the services of a similar company to perform 'twice during each session of equestrian wonders', presumably not at the same time. He also hired a strong-man, Signor Colpi, who supported, on a table held above his head, four men, seven children, and a dog; a turn which is unexplained to this day but which is referred to in the programme bill as 'Some several Magneticall Experiments'; Fortunelly, a clown who not only promised 'to drive grave melanchollie from the heart of the audience' but also took his place among a troupe of acrobats who, standing on each other's shoulders, formed a human pyramid with Fortunelly in cap and bells at the apex; and a number of near-freaks, including a man described as having a 'Cyclops eye' whose eyes were in fact set very close together and with the aid of a little greasepaint could be made to appear close enough to be singular if you viewed him from beyond the barrier specially erected to keep you at a distance.

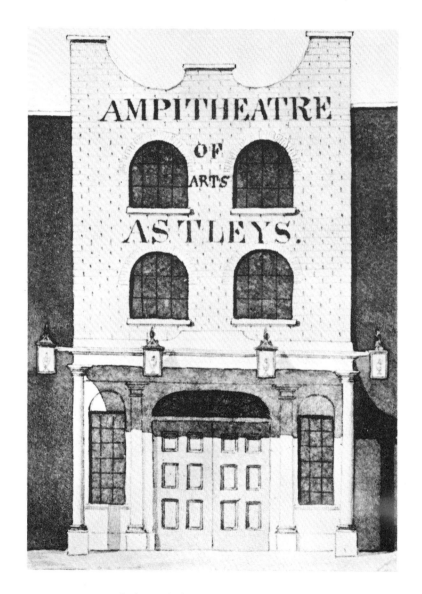

Astley's Amphitheatre of Arts at Westminster.

All these marvels were, of necessity, displayed in the open, in the Halfpenny Hatch field that stretched from the east side of Westminster Bridge to what is now Waterloo Station. There was a tumbledown barn that Astley decided could be a sort of grandstand into which he could put some benches and charge a shilling for a seat thereon – an opportunity that the public took without any reluctance whatever, so that soon the takings mounted to £40 a day, from which he could easily afford to erect a fence round the amphitheatre and keep out the rascals who otherwise would have avoided paying. Also helpful from a publicity angle was a fortuitous visit from George III, who, curious as to the reason for the crowds he saw gathering in Halfpenny Hatch while out for his morning ride, commanded Astley and all his wonders to come and perform before him at Richmond. The esteem that rubbed off on Astley after that command performance was naturally considerable and emboldened him to write what he called 'a small tome' entitled *The Modern Riding Master; or, A Key To The Knowledge Of The Horse and Horsemanship, printed for and sold by the author at his Riding School and Grand Circus, nigh by the bridge at Westminster and the Cut through the Marsh, where admission money will be taken at the Halfpenny Hatch Gate*. The book, which was in fact small (though somewhat longer than its title page), was saucily dedicated to

His Majesty King George ye Third
As your Majesty gives great Encouragement to the breeding and Training of Horses and Horsemanship, and well knowing your Majesty's great Perfection in the Knowledge of that noble and manly Art, made me ambitious of wishing this small Production might appear under your Noble Patronage: not only to add to its lustre, but what an old Soldier values most, the Sanction of his Royal Master.

The book sold well, though it said virtually nothing new about the training of *Equus* and was written in sentences so syntactically involved that they were often impossible of resolution. The purchasers made no complaint, however. They assumed they were being blinded by superior knowledge like those who beheld the emperor's new non-clothes; and when Astley published another book, *Natural Magic*, which was a straight plagiaristic lift from a treatise by the French magician Decremps, *La Magie Blanche Dévoilée*, they assumed Astley had powers

Several of the principal Nobility, now in Town, having solicited Mr. ASTLEY to exhibit the Whole of his Activity on One, Two, Three, and Four Horses, with all his other Amusements, on One Night; therefore gives Notice, that this and every Evening, till Monday next, The grand general Display will be made in a brilliant Manner.

By PARTICULAR DESIRE,
The Whole of these amazing various Exhibitions, under the following Titles, viz.

HORSEMANSHIP, or ACTIVITY,

By Mr. and Mrs. ASTLEY, &c. &c. &c.

The BROAD-SWORD as in Real ACTION.
HEAVY BALLANCING, and Horsemanship BURLESQU'D.
With a COMIC RACE in Sacks, by Four Capital Performers in that Art.

ALSO,

Comus, Jonas, & Breslaw's Tricks, with Sleeve Buttons, Watches, Purses, Money, Letters, Cards, &c.

By the Little Learned MILITARY HORSE.

(With a short instructive Lecture on each by Mr. ASTLEY.)   Also

The Magical Tables: Or, the Little Horse turn'd Conjurer.

In Four GRAND CHANGES.

With Variety of other Exhibitions, to make the General Nights complete.

To begin at a Quarter before Six o'Clock precisely——Admittance One Shilling each, though not the Tenth Part of the Value of such an extraordinary Performance.

*** Mr. ASTLEY has been at a very great Expence in making Preparations for the General Nights, in Order to accommodate the Nobility in an elegant manner, therefore flatters himself, the Variety and Drollness of the several Exhibitions cannot fail of giving the greatest Satisfaction to every Beholder, as there never was a Performance of its Kind at One Place in Europe,

N. B. Mr. Astley thought only to make one General Night, but as the Weather might prove uncertain, and the Night fixed on might not suit every one, and willing to oblige the Nobility, Gentry and others, with such an extraordinary Sight, continues it till Monday next, being positively the last Night.

†§† It is humbly requested the Nobility will be in good Time, in order to see the whole general Display. Servants to keep Places to be at the Door precisely at Four o'Clock, when Mr. Astley will be very punctual in securing such Places as they shall request.

A handbill advertising the
horsemanship of the
Astley family.

beyond the comprehension of normal man. 'How else', asked an awestruck reporter in the *Courant*, 'are we to accompt for Sergeant-Major Astley's success?'

Simply enough, one would have thought: Astley was an opportunist who had answered the knock that had come on his door at exactly the right time; he was a showman-charlatan unequalled until the arrival on the scene of P. T. Barnum; he was an adapter (to put it euphemistically) of other people's ideas and words; and he had all the attributes of a chummy character who could get any message over to the public in their own terms. They, in consequence, would believe almost anything he said – as, for instance, when, sensing the curiosity value of the creature, he bought a crocodile from the anatomist and surgeon John Hunter (who kept a menagerie of exotic animals at Earls Court) and displayed it before the audience, after a great deal of drumming and tucketing to attract attention, with the announcement: 'This 'ere crocudill is the very same one that stopped H'alexander's h'army when it was a-crossing of the Bospuros, and even now, h'after so many years – crocudills being long-living creatures due to their h'appetites – still 'as within its h'intellects the body of a man in h'armour.' His curious historical, geographical, and biological notions were accepted as easily as were his malapropisms, and people crowded to the edge of the Thames to see the strange reptile sunning itself. They also accepted the plain statement that his son, a likely lad who was on horseback almost as soon as he could walk, was five years old 'and the greatest equestrian performer of tender years in the world', when he was ten, and obviously so. The gullibility of the public seems to be without limit so long as their informant has created the right aura about himself and makes his presentation in the right way. Otherwise how could they fall for the small advertisements in the weekend newspapers, the 'easily installed showers that need no complicated plumbing' (but demand the services of the water board, several explosives experts, and the police), the 'fabulously glamorous chandelier made of pure glittering plastic, guaranteed to add beauty and character to any room' (not to mention four carpenters and electricians to fit it), the 'cook-while-u-watch hay-box that costs nothing because it uses nothing but its own power' (and cooks nothing, because nothing in it will ever rise to a higher temperature than sixty degrees – Farenheit at that), the 'slimming wheel you can feel doing

Charles Hughes, one of Astley's employees,
became his rival and established the
Royal Circus at Blackfriars.

you good' (any good you can feel is actually being done to the pocket of the firm that sold it to you), and the 'daring see-through lacy G-string guaranteeing the manly shape that will bring Madame dashing to your side' (where she will take one look and collapse in gales of jeering laughter). Anything whose virtues are set forth in the strange gibberish of the marketeer, whether written or spoken, will find marvelling customers who will subsequently be too ashamed to admit that they have been taken in and that the all-purpose contrivance that was said to relieve tension, adjust sparking-plugs, enable anyone with normal eyesight to see through outer garments to what lies saucily beneath ('What japes you could have in the office!'), and write in twelve different colours ('Even upside down') in the pressurized cabin of a superjet, does not actually relieve tension, adjust sparking-plugs, et cetera. 'Belief', as Shaw makes someone say in *The Doctor's Dilemma*, 'can be produced in practically unlimited quantity and intensity without observation or reasoning, and even in defiance of both by the simple desire to believe founded on a strong interest in believing.' Hence the success of conjurers, advertising agents, and Public Relations men. Not that Astley didn't provide value for money: his own skill alone was enough, and the additional attractions that made up what may be called the embryo of the modern circus provided entertainment for some two hours at modest prices.

It was in the nature of things that his success should arouse envy – and in one of his own performers, no less, a man named Hughes who performed on horseback as startlingly as did Astley, and saw no reason why he should be a mere wage-earner instead of a boss pulling down a fortune. While Astley and his performers were in France entertaining Louis XVI at Versailles at the command of the French Ambassador, Hughes – who had opted out on account of feigned sprains to various limbs – set up a rival establishment by Blackfriars Bridge, which was near enough to be directly competitive with Astley's and offered similar attractions and a more memorable title: The Royal Circus. (Except on the title page of his book, Astley had always called his enterprise a Riding School and Amphitheatre.) The impact made by the simpler name was astonishing. By the time Astley returned his patrons had all found their way to the field farther down the river; worse, he found a magistrate's summons awaiting him for employing 'mountebanks,

A plate, originally hand-coloured,
showing the circus ring, from a
French circus history.

rope-dancers, prize-players, ballad singers, and such as make show of motions and strange sights' without a licence granted by 'Charles Killigrew, Esquire, Master of the Revels to his Majesty'. Presumably Hughes had 'laid an information', though why Astley should not have taken the precaution of obtaining a licence was never explained. What was explained, however, was Astley's unerring success in obtaining one without even answering the summons. He put someone to work for him to unearth information about the office of Master of the Revels, which had been created by Henry VIII, and discovered, *inter alia*, that the Master was also Trumpet-Major of all England and was entitled to receive one penny every time anyone except the trumpeters of the royal household blew a trumpet publicly, 'and therefore has jurisdiction of all the merry-andrews and jack-puddings of every Fair throughout England'. Not only was he boss trumpeter, he was also, as boss reveller, entitled to a seat at any performance of anything given publicly 'even if the place of assembly overfloweth'. Both these privileges had long since been forgotten, and in reminding Mr Killigrew of them and of the comforting little income that could be derived from trumpet blowing a licence was backdated and issued to Astley and the summons withdrawn 'as a mistake'. Astley ceased to use trumpeters forthwith, and concentrated in his fanfares on fifes, flutes, drums, and gongs; but he always kept a seat for Killigrew, who in due course entered into partnership with him in the matter of the construction of a permanent building 'that would add an air of respectability and enable bright light to be used and the grand spectacle of Mazeppa performed, as he had wanted to do for some time', writes Killigrew in his memoirs, 'but could not see his way without there was a proper *theatre of the arts* in which all kinds of performances could be given, and a *circle* round which the audience could congregate and not have to push rudely into one another to gain sight of what was going on – a danger that leads to many fights and women swooning.'

Thus justification for the geometrical shape of the circus came into being. Whether Astley or Hughes was the first to think of the idea it is impossible to establish. As I've said, both resuscitated the word 'circus' after fifteen hundred years – Astley in his book, Hughes as a name for his enterprise. But there is no evidence that at that time Hughes's displays were held in a circular arena; rather,

Astley's new Royal Amphitheatre of the Arts.

such evidence as there is points to them being given, like Astley's, in the manner of a country fair – that is, without much formal organization of the different attractions apart from their being presented serially instead of vying with each other for the attention of the crowds. In fairness, however, one must add that had Hughes had the idea of an encircling audience Astley would have had no compunction about copying it. He was, as I have pointed out, an impenitent snatcher of other men's words and ideas.

At all events, immense building activity began on both the Blackfriars and the Westminster site towards the end of 1778, Hughes having found himself a financial partner in Charles Dibdin, the song writer.* But although there is doubt about who first dreamed up the idea of the circular arena, there is no doubt at all about whose was finished first: Astley's. At the end of 1780 he advertised the opening of 'the magnificent new Amphitheatre in which will be combined all the splendours of Theatre and Fair, with candlelight to Illuminate both stage and arena, upon which will be Performed at the Earliest Opportunity the magnificent Spectacle of Mazeppa, with Master Astley in the principal part, and also many additional attractions never before seen in this country but Gathered by Sergeant-Major Astley (late of the Dragoons) on his tours abroad where he has had the Honour of Performing before his Majesty of France and his Imperial Majesty of Vienna. Among these Marvels will be Those skilled in the Arts of Vaulting, the tremplin, Balancing, prestidigitation, and the Gymnasium – these last to include a Couple who are famous for their marvellous Exertions, in which they extend the body into all sorts of deformed shapes, and stand upon one leg and extend the other Perpendicular half a yard above the head.'

Note, if you will, that Astley still obstinately refused to use the word 'circus' to describe his enterprise; and when, in 1782, Hughes's building was completed and opened as The Royal Circus and Equestrian Philharmonic Academy it was the first three words of that title that continued to appeal more than the cumbrous Amphitheatre of the Arts that Astley insisted on retaining. Curiously, it was not until after Astley's death in 1814 that the obvious ready-made affectionate title of

* Like Schubert, he wrote more than six hundred; but unlike Schubert's they have all been forgotten with the exception of 'Tom Bowling', which has remained in the repertory of ballad singers.

The interior of Astley's Amphitheatre.

'Astley's' was adopted by the general public. The Royal Circus was in common parlance from its very inauguration simply 'The Circus'; Astley's was more awkwardly referred to as 'the Halfpenny Hatch field', 'the Fair along of the Marsh', or 'The Riding School', 'equestrian' and 'amphitheatre' not being words the untutored eye or tongue could easily cope with. (It is worth noting that a good case could have been made out for the transposition of the names, Hughes's enterprise being much stronger on music and ballet, Astley's on what is more easily recognizable as the rumbustious stuff of the circus; but such a transposition could only, of course, have been made in conditions of co-operation, even if it had been thought of.) Whatever the public could or could not cope with in the way of words, however, they knew what they wanted when it came to spectacle: horses, horses, and more horses; daring feats both on and off the horses' backs; a story that made some sort of sense to go with the action; and moments of light banter between an obvious Master of Ceremonies (later to be called the Ringmaster) and the clown (almost universally known in those days as Mr Merryman, rather as the feed man in a nigger minstrel show came to be known as Mr Interlocutor). The banter could be of such inanity that a supposition that the exchange was the drivel of mental vacuity would have been justified. But no matter: it served the purpose of allowing the audience to get its breath back after gasping with excitement. And it also served to introduce a line that has remained in the script of every circus clown since. For when the audience was mopping its collective brow after seeing a representation of a Roman chariot race or the death-defying ride of Mazeppa, or lowering its gaze from the lofty height where some marvellously skilled equilibrist was poised on one hand on the top of a slender pole with his body gracefully curving like a bow into the upper air, they welcomed the relief of tension that ensued when Mr Merryman came bouncing on shouting 'Here we are again!'

The same words might reasonably be echoed by the reader who has three times encountered the name Mazeppa and wonders who he was – or, knowing Byron's bouncy narrative poem or Pushkin's play *Pultowa*, wonders equally how Astley came to be toying with the idea of Mazeppa's ride before either Byron or Pushkin had seen the light of day. (Byron was born in 1788, Pushkin in 1799, and

Preparing for Mazeppa's Ride. An illustration by
John Tenniel, *Punch*, 1851.

their creations on the subject of Mazeppa were published in 1819 and 1828 respectively.) The answer is that everyone was toying with the tale, if not with the idea of presenting it live, so to speak. It had captured the romantic fancy of tale-bearers, of whom in all ages there are plenty. (Take the present-day folk yarn of the family living on Kit-e-Kat, or the one about the lady whose trailing dress caught in the trouser zip of the man she was pressing past in the theatre.) And the tale-bearers had passed it on across the steppes of Russia to Europe, where, embroidered in the translation and by the whims of those telling it, it had been printed many times in doggerel verse and crude prose, and even set to music (by Charles Dibdin). It lent itself easily to romantic elaboration and it certainly got it. The hero of the tale was Ivan Mazeppa, a Pole of noble family who in the middle of the seventeenth century became a page to the king of Poland. All might have been well with his progress through the protocol of the court had he not foolishly seduced Theresia, the young wife of one of his betters in the hierarchy, and, even more foolishly, allowed the intrigue to be discovered. The cuckolded husband, enraged at finding Mazeppa naked in Theresia's bed, ordered that he be tied naked to the back of a wild horse which would then be turned loose. Wild horses do not take kindly to such liberties, and it was a reasonable supposition that Mazeppa would die of exposure combined with the considerable torture he would suffer as a result of the horse's terrified flight over the plains. But in fact the horse, exhausted, ended its wild gallop near a Cossack encampment, and Mazeppa was released and cared for by the soldiers. His aristocratic origins being plain to all, he was given officer status and in time so distinguished himself that he became a prince of the Ukraine at the court of Peter the Great.

There is about the tale, as you see, everything to appeal to those who sympathize with the underdog and cheer when the villain (even though his villainy may to some extent be justified) is thwarted in his designs. That particular satisfaction, though, was more muted than the cheers that were raised at the excitement of the spectacle itself, which was managed with as much aplomb as would be expected today in a Drury Lane presentation. The stage that formed part of the arena was brilliantly lit by three chandeliers, each fitted with, it was said, five hundred candles. The proscenium revealed a bleak scene cunningly contrived

ASTLEY'S

ROYAL AMPHITHEATRE OF ARTS.
Proprietor & Manager, Mr, WILLIAM BATTY, Bridge Road, Lambeth, Surrey
LICENSED BY THE LORD HIGH CHAMBERLAIN.

GRAND **SPECTACLE**

EXTRAORDINARY!

CONTINUED SUCCESS OF MAZEPPA!
FOR SIX NIGHTS LONGER!

In compliance to the demand for places to witness MAZEPPA, and on account of the Extensive Preparations for the New Military Spectacle, Lord Byron's magnificent Drama of the **Wild Horse** will be **repeated for**

A playbill advertising Mazeppa's Ride at Astley's.

so that the horse bearing the hero appeared to ascend through mountainous country and diminish into the distance – an effect that was managed by stage-hands moving bits of scenery and scrim to result in the equivalent of the cinema's 'dissolves'. The early scene of Mazeppa's discovery in the arms and the bed of Theresia was acted out in silhouette behind a gauze, this discreet method of over-coming what Sergeant-Major Astley called 'an h'indelicate situation' being fully approved 'by licence of the Lord High Chamberlain', or so the playbill said. But Mazeppa was later dragged into the ring wearing nothing but pink fleshings and a diagonal sash like the ribbon of a noble order carefully arranged to run con-cealingly between his legs, ladies in the audience being very coy about such a revealing costume and making a great to-do of hiding their blushes while simul-taneously widening their eyes. Anyway, lashed by fierce varlets to the back of the horse, Mazeppa's ride began, increasing in speed as the horse circled the ring three times, and at a signal from the rider leapt upon the stage and at full gallop continued up the spirally-arranged track into the scenic distance, only to emerge, minutes later, in the brilliantly transformed scene of the Cossack's camp. More front-of-curtain stuff in which his adult life was chopped into convenient miniature scenes like a triptych, then a splendid finale in which, arrayed in princely style, he reviewed the Tsar's troops, whose horses gracefully fell to their knees as he passed before them on the now tamed mount on which he had been so cruelly dispatched onto the steppes.

The original Astley version was changed countless times, becoming in one way or another more sensational each time, particularly after Byron renewed interest in the tale with his narrative poem, which elaborated it by having Mazeppa tell his story to Charles XII of Sweden (to whom he had defected from the Russians) after the battle of Pultowa. The most sensational version didn't appear until long after the Sergeant-Major had quipped his last quip with Mr Merryman and died, in 1814, at the Cirque Olympique in Paris, which he had established. It was the version presented by that woman so much given to sensation, Ada McCord, who acquired a Jewish husband (one of an uncertain number of spouses) named Alexander Isaac Menken and thereafter, despite the several husbands who suc-ceeded him, kept his name and his faith and called herself Adah Isaacs Menken.

Adah Isaacs Menken, as Mazeppa.

She would have made a good wife for Baron Munchausen – insofar as she would have made a good wife for anybody – for they could have vied with each other in the enormity of the lies they told. To the extent that anything at all can be established about her, she was born a Creole, possibly but by no means certainly in the West Indies, in 1835. She learnt to ride by getting a job at Franconi's circus when it was in New York, married a stable boy when still in her teens, divorced him as quickly as was legally possible, learnt dancing and got in the *corps de ballet* at the Opera House, Mexico City, invented an astonishing story about being captured by Red Indians, and settled into the arms of Menken, who taught her, *inter alia*, singing. Adopting the tenets of Judaism easily enough, she nevertheless refused to give up smoking – a habit Alexander would not tolerate. Presumably there was a divorce, for she soon married a young boxer and stayed married to him from April to September 1859, when she became an actress at the New York National Theater and put herself into print as 'the poetess of the new age' (paying for publication, naturally) and 'the only actress and authoress in the school of American Thespianism who regularly entertains the most enthusiastic audiences with her readings from Shakespeare given from the back of an Arab steed'. She also (she said) danced 'the dances of many nations' – though whether while reading Shakespeare from the back of the Arab steed is not clear. Evidently she seized upon other people's ideas as easily as Astley had done; for, having heard that a horsewoman named Charlotte Crampton was attracting big audiences for 'the most intrepid feats ever performed by a lady on Horseback, including the Wild Ride of Prince Mazeppa', she decided she would outride Miss Crampton and present a version of Mazeppa even more intrepid. The intrepidity, she said, would lie in the fact that she would be naked upon the back of her horse, as Mazeppa had been, 'and lacking which nudity the tale is false'. (She said nothing about the greater falsity of a female Mazeppa.) There was a lot of fuss in the papers about her 'undressing', but in those days any woman who so much as showed an ankle in public was considered fast; and if she appeared on a public stage with her throat and thighs visible there would be shrieks from the vigilantes. The only picture of Adah in her Mazeppa get-up shows her artistically but impractically poised on a fierily rearing horse wearing a quasi-Greek garment that apart from revealing

A cartoon portraying Menken as Mazeppa
from *La Lune*, Paris, 1867.

her left shoulder and her knees is of the utmost decorum. That she ever appeared naked except in some seedy saloon is about as probable as that she was the *friend* (she always put the word in italics to give it extra significance) of Charles Dickens and the mistress of Swinburne, both of which liaisons she claimed.

Having found but small success with her Mazeppa venture in New York, she huffily published some scathing verse – much of which was a juxtaposition of lines lifted directly from Whitman – and sailed for England in a clipper. There she was taken in hand by E. T. Smith, 'the English Barnum', sometime manager of Drury Lane, with a finger in a great many pies, including a brothel or two, a millinery shop at Brighton, a supper-room in the vaults of the Royal Exchange, and a directorial interest in Astley's, the rebuilding of which he'd helped finance after it had been burnt down in 1803. Adah paraded before him in her Mazeppa costume and he put her under contract at once. Pulling all the strings that could be caught at with the help of a sovereign or two, Smith created a sensational background for her to appear against before she'd even left her hotel 'on a secret visit to Dumas in his rooms in the Rue Saint-Honoré, Paris'. Her likeness by Sir John Tenniel appeared in *Punch*; sandwich-board men and hired hansoms plastered with posters trundled through the streets of London calling attention to the forthcoming 'Grand Spectacle Drama of The Wild Horse ridden IN THE FLESH ! ! ! by the famous actress and equestrienne Adah Isaacs Menken'; writers of puffs in the press wrote gossipy bits that implied frightful goings-on in the life of the equestrienne; the names of Swinburne and Dickens were mentioned in a manner just short of libellous; and professional whisperers whispered it abroad that 'Royalty' were among her patrons, though what royalty and in what manner their patronage had been extended was left to the listeners' imaginations, deliberately. The effect of the buildup was roughly the same as might be gained by sensational plugs at peak-time viewing on today's television; and after several weeks of it, to quote Mr Maurice Willson Disher in *Clowns and Pantomimes*:

> Astley's doors opened on October 3rd, 1864, to admit a vast press of spectators, who could barely restrain their impatience while a curtain-raiser called *The Double-Bedded Room* was being played. So well had Smith done his work that there was an outbreak of applause at Menken's first appearance, though she was completely dressed (as the Tartar captive,

A drawing by Tenniel of the Tartar hordes at Astley's.

disguised as the page of the Polish Castellan). After declaiming each line with a strong foreign accent, she struck a pose 'as if with the view of satisfying an audience of photographers'. But in the scene where Mazeppa marched into the apartments of the Count Palatine to fight him for the love of Olinska, the Castellan's daughter (nothing so immoral as the unfaithful wife of Byron's poem had ever been tolerated at Astley's), Menken dropped her attitudinizing and fought with 'wonderful vigour and spirit' until the would-be bridegroom was overcome.

Here the audience held its breath in exquisite anticipation. The Castellan was about to wreak his vengeance by ordering 'the punishment inflicted on rebel slaves'. First Mazeppa must be stripped. This was the great moment of the play. Menken retained, of course, the tight fleshings that had been properly worn by previous Mazeppas in this situation, but instead of the usual dark brown 'half-body' she had loose folds of white linen which descended 'only slightly towards the knee', and left the upper limb exposed, though not indelicately. Some spectators might murmur, 'Not the sort of thing one would care one's sister to see', but others had been educated by Smith into thinking, not of their sister, but of the ladies of ballet or burlesque. Only a very small minority were bold enough to observe that the Mazeppa on Astley's stage was better clothed than those of the hoardings: all watched the binding with many a thong of hero to horse breathlessly, and shuddered as they saw both rush over the raking platforms, followed by the heads of wolves with moveable jaws . . . worked by stage-hands who crawled, concealed by the painted canvas parapet, carefully behind the clattering hoofs, in order to represent the stealing, rustling step of that 'long gallop, which can tire / The Hound's deep fate and hunter's fire.' When the long top platform of the stage (there were three) had been passed, cardboard figures of diminishing sizes continued the flight 'to stretch beyond the night'.

The curtain fell amid cheers, and Menken was twice led forward by Smith. In the next act she posed to represent Mazeppa's gradual awakening, amid a snow-clad landscape, from the recollections of his fearful ride to the comprehension of his present safety among the Tartars of his father, the Abder Khan. To give vent to his rejoicings and once more assuming the 'god-like attitude of freedom and man', she armed herself with sword and shield and struck a series of poses 'taken from the most celebrated sculptures of antiquity'. On the abdication of the Abder Khan in Mazeppa's favour, she bestrode the wild horse in masculine fashion, and, after marshalling her troops (Astley's stud of forty horses and company of two hundred performers), she responded to a clamorous recall by waving her acknowledgements from the saddle.

All good stuff, as you see, and with a touch of Women's Lib about it. The vast press of spectators loved it and would have kept it going long beyond

Astley's acrobats in Paris.

Christmas if the pantomime of *Harlequin Jack Sprat; or, The Three Blind Mice, Great A, Little A, and Bonny B, the Cat's In The Cupboard And She Can't See Me* hadn't been scheduled. Adah's act combined the best elements of circus, fair, and theatre. Her raffish private life – if private it could be called – was as impermanent as that of any itinerant wanderer; her revealing costume, though somewhat less revealing than by implication promised, was an important step towards leotard and spangles; her histrionics, though by today's standards extremely hammy, had about them the roll of drums that announces a hair-raising event; and her willingness to be manipulated by impresarios and surrounded by sensation was the very stuff of what was later to be called by one of its dominant impresarios The Greatest Show On Earth. In short, she had drawn together the threads gathered up by Astley, who, earlier, had shrewdly grasped at the leftovers from the palmy days of Rome – the Big Top, the equestrian spectacle, the wire-walkers and rope-dancers and clowns and exotic and performing animals – and melded them into an entertainment that excited and pleased all ages and all classes. More, she had introduced and made acceptable the idea of women other than actresses being entertainers in a field that had hitherto been exclusively male.

A handbill advertising Madame Zazel.

4.

... and the Girls

IN THE DAYS OF MY DEVOTION TO THE IDEA OF A CIRCUS INFORMATION BUREAU one of the most cherished of the bits of *memorabilia* that decorated my bedroom was a handbill, printed on the coarse paper used for the yard-long sheets of songs sold by ballad-mongers, advertising the sensational Madame Zazel, who nightly 'except on Sundays and holy days' was fired 'from a monstrous cannon' over the heads of the gaping audience at West's Amphitheatre – a place that for a time rivalled Astley's. The machine was not, of course, a cannon but a spring-loaded catapult; equally, Zazel was not a Madame but a Miss Napper who came from Leicester and was pictured in the crude block that illustrated the leaflet as a busty lady wearing what appeared to be a corset and buttoned leggings. Her attitude in the drawing was one of victory: one arm was raised above her head and a smudgy smirk lit her features – as well it might, for every time she described her parabola over the heads of the audience and landed in her safety net she received £20. In 1877, when she first submitted to being stuffed down the barrel of the machine, with a great deal of playful ramrodding by stage assistants and startled cries from the audience as a percussion cap was fired at the business end simultaneously with the release of the catapult springs, that was big money. It was probably ten times as much as the majority of the members of her audience each earned in a week. But the lives of ladies fired into the air from cannons are at some hazard. (So are the lives of trawler-men and miners; but their activities are not attractive to others, and anyway they are not susceptible of assembly in an auditorium.) Quite apart from that, though, the very fact that she was a woman was sensational enough in itself. Since Adah Isaacs Menken there had been no feminine sensationalism in show business. A few equestriennes had appeared at Franconi's circus in Paris and Juan Porte's in Vienna;

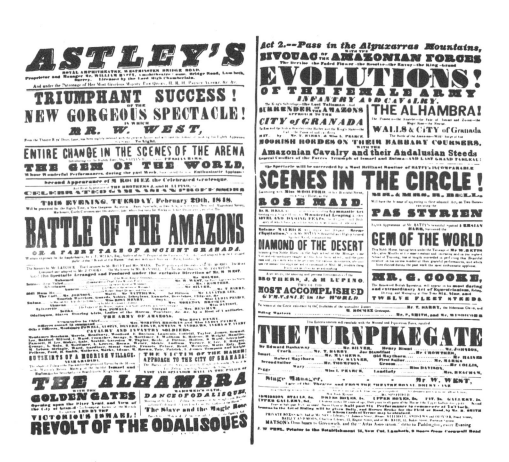

A bill advertising the spectaculars of
Astley's Circus, 1848.

Astley's own Cirque Olympique had featured a strong-woman; Rickett's in Philadelphia had had a welcoming committee of bluestocking ladies when Washington had visited it in 1792, but they scarcely counted as sensational; and among the performers at the Russian circus in St Petersburg had been a troupe of ballet girls. None of these attracted much attention, for apart from the strong-woman they did nothing remarkable; and even the strong-woman did no more than toy with some dumb-bells, then a new-fangled contrivance of which the weight, it was recognized, could well be illusory. Audiences like the freakish, the odd, the daring, the astonishing, the unbelievable that must be believed because the evidence is before the very eyes. It was daring (in more ways than one) to be lashed naked – even if the nakedness was implied rather than real – to the back of a horse which then enacted a real-life drama with a satisfying pay-off. It was wonderful to become a human cannon-ball, whichever sex you were; but for the frailer of the two it was nothing short of miraculous. That the tender feminine body could stand such treatment night after night! There were whispers that Madame Zazel was in league with the devil, to whom she had bartered her soul for some unseemly purpose such as the achievement of material gain, and that a few years earlier she would have been burnt at the stake as a witch. But whatever her private arrangements with subterranean forces, she received the wild plaudits of the crowd, who probably felt a certain amount of audience participation because it was across their heads that she flew and on to their heads that she would fall if a mishap occurred. But there were no mishaps. She completed her two-year stint and retired on what was left of her £12,480 – a considerable amount since she was frugal – to live a sheltered life at Ashby de la Zouch. So sheltered was her life that she was virtually a recluse, and lay dead for three days before a visiting dairymaid who brought her farm produce discovered her body. Whether her soul ever went to the devil was never established, or even bothered about. She whizzed over the ducked heads of the marvelling audience and then whizzed no more. End of story.

Miss Napper's name is buried in the annals; Jules Léotard's lives on, largely because he took the precaution of bestowing his name on an article of apparel, just as Cardigan, Ulster, and Wellington did. The leotard is the standard body-stocking costume still worn by gymnasts and trapeze artistes, of whom Léotard was the first

The American Circus at the Alhambra Palace.

to fly through the air from one trapeze to another. Like Zazel he was a whizzer, and when, in 1859, after a lot of swinging to and fro to gain momentum, he released his hold on his trapeze and whizzed over the ring of the Cirque Napoléon in Paris to grab safely at a matching trapeze twenty feet away, the audience screamed first with apprehension and then with delight and admiration. Trapezists they had seen many times, but flying trapezists never. The newspaper report of his act was picked up by the London *Observer*, and a representative of the Alhambra in Leicester Square, which had just opened as a permanent circus, went post-haste to Paris to book him. Duly booked, he went to London, flew through the air with the greatest of ease (words that were incorporated in a song about him called 'The Daring Young Man on the Flying Trapeze', which was sung by the music hall star George Leybourne and is still performed today), to the somewhat more blasé applause of Londoners. It wasn't that they didn't appreciate the skill, timing, and courage of Léotard; rather, their collective minds were filled with notions gained from the advance publicity generated by the agents of the American showman Phineas T. Barnum, who had launched Jenny Lind, 'The Swedish Nightingale', and had an ever-changing collection of grotesques and marvels that had been presented 'to all the principal Courts of Europe' and included midgets ('General' Tom Thumb), white Negroes, 'monster snakes', Ethiopian minstrels, giants and giantesses, double-voiced singers, leviathans and behemoths (whales and hippopotamuses), mermaids, and the 'remarkable Woolly Horse which is made up of Elephant, Deer, Horse, Buffalo, Camel and Sheep, has the haunches of a deer, the tail of an elephant, a fine curled wool coat of camel's hair colour, and easily bounds twelve or fifteen feet high'. Impatience for the arrival of such curiosities perhaps lessened the impact of a mere man flying through the air, and the proprietors of the Alhambra, who had hoped that Léotard would establish the success of their newly opened circus, were disappointed. The enterprise failed, and success came to the building only when it was reopened as a music hall and, ironically, echoed to the words of 'The Daring Young Man' ('Sung with ever increasing popularity by Mr George Leybourne, arranged in three keys –: viz, E, F, and G, and obtainable from the publishers post free'). But the audiences were different.

The people waiting for woolly horses and Ethiopian minstrels had seen cunningly

Sketches of Barnum's show at Olympia, 1889.

sited advance notices proclaiming in huge letters WAIT FOR BARNUM. DON'T SPEND YOUR MONEY ON INFERIOR SHOWS. 'Inferior shows' referred especially to Cooper & Bailey's Circus, whose rivalry with Barnum was so intense that in America the Bailey of the concern had once ordered the destruction of a bridge after his company had passed over it, so that Barnum would have to take a circuitous route and would thereby miss the business in the town both were aiming for. Below the admonition to wait for Barnum was the inducement:

> Come from your fields, your workshops, your offices, your stores and homes! Gather your
> families – your friends – your neighbours, and make a holiday for once! Secure an eligible
> position by 9 o'clock in the morning, and see the gorgeous procession – then troop along to
> the acres of snowy canvas, and devote the rest of the day to seeing my Grand Museum, my
> School of Automatic Wonders, the Tattooed Greek Nobleman, Giants and Dwarfs, my
> Gigantic Menagerie, my Twenty Trained Imported Stallions, and my Magnificent Circus!
> Then you can go home happy, having enjoyed yourselves innocently and learned much
> that will afford you pleasure hereafter. Then for a night's refreshing sleep and a good day's
> work tomorrow.

All these promised marvels divided those who were, so to speak, Barnum people from those who were happy enough to remain Léotard people. But the Barnum people were not to be gratified as quickly as they thought. The great showman was enduring a misfortune: he had been bankrupted by a confidence trick played on him by someone, never identified, in the Jerome Clock Company of New Haven, Connecticut, to whom he had been induced to give signed promissory notes for more than half a million dollars to save the firm from ruin. No such salvation had come about and Barnum's notes had been called in, thus ruining him.

Barnum, who delighted in the title Prince of Humbugs bestowed on him by James Gordon Bennett, owner of the *New York Herald*, established himself as an impresario when he launched the New York Museum of Marvels and Curiosities From All Parts of the Globe. Advertising and a gullible public had ensured his success. He had genuine oddities such as the midget Charles Stratton, who became under Barnum's management General Tom Thumb and during a tour of England was invited to Windsor by Queen Victoria; he had an aquarium with dolphins and

Jumbo, the African elephant at the Zoological
Gardens, was purchased by T. P. Barnum for
his circus.

a small whale that were real enough; he had orang-utans and he had bell ringers who were allegedly Swiss but in fact came from Liverpool, though they too were real enough. But the shouting and ballyhoo were all for his phoney exhibits – the 'Feejee Mermaid preserved', which was in fact a plaster model kept like the 'Cyclops eye' at a distance that didn't permit of close examination; 'The Oldest Living Woman, Joice Heth, aged 161 years, once a Slave in the Household of George Washington's father', who following an autopsy performed after her death was proved to be no more than eighty; and the 'Cardiff Giant', supposedly the remains of a prehistoric man excavated in New York but in fact no more than a manufactured skeleton. When his falsifications were revealed Barnum delighted in the publicity and pointed out that it is possible to fool only those who are willing to be fooled or who haven't the wit to tell true from false. To prove it he put up a notice above a staircase in the museum with an arrow pointing 'To The Egress' and watched scornfully as people hastened down the stairs only to find themselves in the street. He had been taught show business by Aaron Turner, a man who ran a small travelling circus of sorts and who emphasized the value of notoriety and the spending of big sums of money – even if it was non-existent or borrowed money – to bring in yet bigger sums. Barnum's brief partnership with Turner was unsuccessful but he never forgot the value of publicity. Until the financial débâcle caused by the failure of the clock company, his life as an impresario was wholly successful and he made and spent fortunes, lived a godly, righteous, and sober life (or was seen so to live, which amounted to the same thing), and never let an opportunity pass or a day go by without gaining his share of public attention. When bankruptcy had him in its grip he repaid many of his debts by lecturing all over America and Europe on 'The Art of Money-Getting', a subject so ludicrous for one in his position that it transcended the bounds of absurdity and alighted on the pinnacle of realism. When the American Museum was burnt down in 1865 he had it rebuilt within four months; and when it was burnt down again in 1868 he sold the right to use his name to a rival museum proprietor called George Wood in exchange for three per cent of Wood's receipts, determining to retire from public life and devote himself to good works. But the only good works Barnum's nature inclined to were those involving activity and the making of money, and he gave a number

Jumbo refused to leave the Zoo.

of popular lectures on the Christian faith of Universalism, which he embraced without quite knowing what it meant except that its tenets would absolve him from any possibility of hellfire for the many frauds he had perpetrated. At a hundred dollars a time, plus all expenses, he could have done worse, particularly as he and his audiences were equally hazy about Universalism, with or without hellfire. But the roar of the greasepaint and the smell of the crowd were missing; Barnum found his own piety as boring as that of the people who came to hear him. 'My energies', he wrote in his voluminous autobiography, 'were unassuaged by travel and lecturing and insisted upon a wider outlet. I felt the attraction of public power when I visited Salt Lake City and offered Mr Brigham Young, President of the Mormons, half the guaranteed receipts of $200,000 per year if he would allow me to exhibit him and his many wives in New York; but still there was no satisfaction in my heart at such a passive enterprise, and despite my earlier determination to retire I found myself thinking of pastures new.'

The pastures in which he found himself were not altogether new: he had trodden them before with Aaron Turner. But this time his partners, William Coup and Dan Costello, were by no means small-time circus proprietors: 'They had a show', Barnum tells us, 'that was truly immense and combined all the elements of museum, menagerie, variety performance, concert hall, and circus. They came to me for financial help and advice and I was willing, indeed anxious, to supply both – for here, I saw, was something that had the potency to become The Greatest Show on Earth – for so I decided it should be dubbed.' For sheer size, expressed in acreage of canvas and number of performers and employees, there was no doubt about its being the Greatest, and Barnum – who naturally was in charge of publicity – made as much play with figures and superlatives as Hollywood's publicity men were to make for the epics of the screen in the twenties and thirties. (Hal Wallis, a publicist at Warner Brothers, said in a newspaper article, 'We all took our cue from Barnum and Bailey.') He claimed a total of four thousand employees, performers, and animals, thirty-two acres of canvas, 'three tons of sawdust used at every venue', and 'field kitchens that were used in the recent disturbances [presumably the Civil War] to prepare the provender, to provide which costs $200,000 per week, man and beast'. The list of attractions included equestrian teams

French acrobats performing.

'outshining all those that have performed in the history of the world, not excepting amid the grandeur of Imperial Rome', Anna Leake the Armless Woman, automata that 'at the will of the beholder will breathe in lifelike fashion and gasp for breath if told to do so', some allegedly man-eating cannibals from Fiji, Admiral Dot the Eldorado Elf and Colonel Goshen the Palestinian Giant, the Sleeping Beauty and the Dying Zouave (a euphonious working name, true, but what can they have done if one was sleeping and the other dying?), giraffes, elephants, and the rest of the exotic menagerie, together with waxworks, dioramas, fountains with no visible source of supply, and a team of wire-walkers, equilibrists, conjurers, clowns, jugglers, trampoline performers, prima donnas, ballad singers, musicans, and 'in every town visited a Grand Parade with full band to be seen absolutely free prior to the erecting of the numerous tents, together with the cavalcade of wagons and machinery that in their amazing plenitude cannot but be recognized as the components of The Greatest Show on Earth'.

Greatest or not, the show did not satisfy Barnum – mainly because there was a rival circus, Cooper & Bailey's, that was taking more money. Its fortune had been made because it had a baby elephant that had been born within its purlieus – the first ever born in captivity. Zoologists were afire with enthusiasm and their word-of-mouth recommendation took thousands to Cooper & Bailey's whose patronage Barnum knew could be his if he played his cards right. After a great many diplomatic, or, as some called them, snaky, lunges, during the course of which Cooper conveniently died, Barnum came to a partnership agreement with Bailey – an agreement that was announced to the accompaniment of screaming publicity. But it was still not enough for Barnum, who thought 'Greatest' a superlative capable of infinite expansion. And if it wasn't practical to enlarge the cast of characters, why not enlarge the stage? In other words, give the customers twice as much to look at for their money, in *two* rings instead of one. From that it was but a step to even greater value and a three-ring circus. But although the idea of triple value appealed to people to begin with, it was quickly found that only one spectacle at a time could be watched, so that as far as value was concerned they were back at what might be called ring one. Though the three-ring circus was for a time made much of in the United States, it achieved what was literally transitory fame

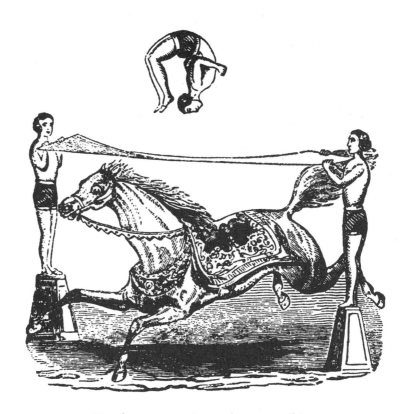

Woodcut: an equestrian acrobat somersaulting.

based on the buildup presaging its arrival in each town and the disappointment it left behind. Elsewhere it was taken to be a mere manifestation of the American craze for gigantism and never made the grade. 'It's a contradiction in terms', Bernard Shaw remarked, 'like saying that a pianist has the fingers of a flying angel when he's playing the Mephisto Waltz'. All the same, the term has sunk into the language as a synonym for anything wild and confusing. No doubt Barnum, peering out from his haven of Universalism, is satisfied with that small addition to his fame. If not – and it was not in his nature to be easily satisfied, as we have seen – let him top the confection of his notoriety with this whipping from Eric Partridge's *Name Into Word:*

> **Barnumism; barnumize,** transitive. (To subject to) advertisement or talk that is showy, boastful, bombastic – pretentious ballyhoo. From Phineas Taylor Barnum (1810–91), American showman, who became famous in the U.S.A. in 1842, in Britain several years later; in 1871 opened at Brooklyn 'The Greatest Show on Earth'; in 1881 combined with Bailey to form the Barnum & Bailey Circus; remained in the circus business until his death.

It is not given to many to be enshrined in an Eric Partridge word book as both a noun and a transitive verb.

LORD GEORGE SANGER'S

GREAT

London and Continental Circus,

DALSTON JUNCTION

General Business Manager	...	...	...	**MR. A. OLLIVER.**
Equestrian Director	...	...	**MR. JAMES HOLLOWAY**
Musical Director	...	...	...	... **MR. SCHOTZ.**

Programme.

SUBJECT TO ALTERATIONS

1. Selection by the Band.
2. Bros. **LA PLACE**, Graceful Performance on the Revolving Globe.
3. **H. AUSTIN**, in his great Hurdle Act.
4. **LARNO & ALLO**, in their Comical Boxing Act.
5. **HERR ULRIC**, in his Great Barrel Performance in mid-air
6. **Mdlle. CAROLINE**, in her Great Scene Act as Joan of Arc.   Clown **LINWOOD**.
7. Comic Entree **LINWOOD**.
8. **ARMSTRONG** the Fool.
9. Olympian Revels by the Bros. **AUSTIN**.
10. **LITTLE HURST** and his Magic Chairs.
11. Shaw the Life Guardsman by **R. YELDING**.

Interval of Ten Minutes.

12. The **YEVEYS**, in their great Musical Act.
13. **Mdlle. LILIAN**, the Graceful Equestrienne.

Clown the Great **JAMES HOLLOWAY**.

14. The Great **JAMES HOLLOWAY** and his Comical Mule.
15. **KATIE GILBERT**, in her Graceful mid-air Performances.
16. **NITRA PALMYRA**, in her Lightning Hurdle Act.
17. Professor **JAMES**, the Ladder Fiend.
18. **GEO. AUSTIN**, the Demon Jockey.   Clown **LITTLE HURST**.
19. Entree **LITTLE HURST**.
20. Vaulting, or Trial of Skill by the Members of the Company
21. **GOD SAVE THE QUEEN**

Printed by Stigant & How, "Hackney Standard" Office, Clapton.

The programme for Lord George Sanger's
Circus at Dalston, 1896.

5.

Big Tops and Little Tops

TRACING CIRCUS GENEALOGY IS IN A WAY SIMILAR TO FOLLOWING ONE OF those genealogical chapters of begattery in the Old Testament. Turner begat Barnum, Barnum begat Bailey, Bailey begat Sanger, Sanger begat Ringling – the trunk branches off into Hagenbecks and Bostocks, Recos and Chipperfields and Smarts, Millses, Lloyds, Cottles, Yeldings, Garrards and Wombwells and Cookes and Codys and Fossetts... the branches diminish into tendrils, and around the time of summer bank holidays in the provinces and suburbs you may well encounter, in a meadow near a river, the garishly painted wagons of a new shoot, a name unheard of but by no means shy with the adjectives 'Tremendous', 'Great', 'Remarkable', 'Unique'. Circus lights are not to be hidden under bushels. Nor are circus proprietors averse from raising themselves above their station in the social hierarchy. Both the Sangers, George and John, styled themselves Lords, Robert Fossett gave himself a knighthood, William Cody (Buffalo Bill) publicized himself as The Honorable, which was indicative only of his membership of the Nebraska Legislature, not his status in the English peerage, and Ohmy the acrobat, who ran his own circus, made no bones about calling himself King Ohmy. The custom arose from a court case in 1887, when George Sanger was sued by Cody for describing part of the Sanger circus as 'The Wild West' – a title Cody had created and not unnaturally didn't want anyone else using. He won the day, Mr Justice Charles issuing an injunction to prevent Sanger 'passing off' any part of his show as a 'Wild West' entertainment or using the words 'Buffalo Bill'. Sanger was furious. His grandson, telling us about it, says: 'What had rankled quite as much as the Court's decision was the constant reiteration during the proceedings of the phrase "The Honorable William Cody".... My grandfather banged his

Scenes at Sanger's Circus, 1886.

fist on the table with a force that made all the cups rattle and exclaimed "The Honorable William Cody! If that Yankee bugger can be an Honorable, then I shall be a Lord!" And from that moment he was.'

Cody, whose show was for the most part what we would now call a rodeo, had become a Pony Express rider when at the age of fifteen he had answered a newspaper advertisement:

WANTED – Young, skinny, wiry fellows not over 18. Must be expert riders willing to risk death daily. Orphans preferred.

He remained with the mail service, risking death daily, until, on 26 October 1861, another notice appeared in the newspapers: PONY EXPRESS WILL BE DISCONTINUED FROM THIS DATE. Cody then went into the army and served as a scout and guide in the Civil War and when that was over got involved with the construction of the Kansas Pacific Railway, for whose navigators he undertook to supply buffalo meat. In eighteen months the undertaking cost the lives of 4,820 buffalo, all of which Cody shot personally. 'Buffalo Bill' was hardly a misnomer, and when in 1883 Cody started his travelling Wild West show he adopted it, Barnum-wise, as his publicity gimmick. 'The Great Buffalo Bill and his Amazing Wild West Show': it would be unthinkable to eschew the adjectives, unthinkable that anything or anyone in a travelling show of any kind could be anything but amazing. Audiences become blasé, but artistes are always one step ahead of them. Léotard's twenty-foot flight through the air in 1859 was soon beaten in terms of distance and daring. Double back somersaults in flight between the two trapezes became common; then, when that failed to arouse any special excitement, came triple back somersaults. The impossible was achieved in mid-air; trapezists and rope-walkers balanced head to head on a swinging bar; they twiddled like catherine wheels for seemingly endless moments before landing apparently effortlessly on their feet on a swinging trapeze. They walk upside down along horizontal rope ladders stretched between the king-poles of the Big Top; they balance themselves in a column four bodies high on a thin wire forty feet above the ring with nothing to catch them if they fall but the inhospitable ground below; they achieve human pyramids five layers high, fragile as a house of cards; there is no end to the ingenuity with which

A performing elephant at Astley's,
late nineteenth century.

they think of, and achieve, new contortions of their bodies, no end to the miracles that can be performed on bicycles and monocycles and on horseback and with chairs. 'With what object', wrote one unimpressed critic in 1965, 'do six men balance upside down on a lopsided tower of six chairs, the back legs of each chair being, in turn, balanced on the outer edge of the seat of the chair just beneath it?' If the question was not merely rhetorical I would have thought the object was to prove the peak of physical perfection to which the human body can be brought and the extent to which the laws of nature can be trifled with; not to mention the earning of money.

Money. All acrobats and equilibrists are paid as highly as their attraction to the crowds underwrites their demands. If they are not permanently contracted to a particular showman there are continual out-bidding offers to tempt them away from wherever they are. Nowadays tours are arranged for them by agents, as for concert artistes, and they may be in Moscow one week, London the next, Melbourne the next. But the main difficulty about travelling is that it leaves little time and no opportunity for the continuous practice that is essential. High-wire acts cannot be accomplished in aeroplanes, though motor-way service areas may provide temporary practice grounds for acrobats. Not long ago travellers on a German autobahn were astonished to see a young man in a spangled leotard standing behind a motor-way garage holding before him a twelve-foot steel pole up which a slender, pretty girl rapidly climbed. At the top she seized short transverse handles and gracefully inverted her body. Her partner then raised the pole with the upside-down girl on it above his shoulders and balanced it on his forehead. The man who told me about this was in the audience beside me when I watched the same couple go faultlessly through the same routine in Billy Smart's circus at its winter quarters in Windsor. That was in November 1976 and the Big Top was full of television equipment recording the show for screening on Christmas Day. He was an elderly man and he recalled a visit to Paris by the Acrobatic Theatre of China, which is sponsored by the People's Republic as an export. 'They juggle, of course – those innumerable plates spinning ceaselessly at the end of sticks – and they bounce on trampolines and get their bodies interlocked in apparently inextricable knots, all of which one has seen before a hundred times. But the

Blondin eating his dinner on the rope
at the Crystal Palace, 1861.

Chinese do these things and countless others with a degree of perfection that is unbelievable. It is beautiful, the very perfection of it; but you could say also that it is in a way mechanical because of the effortlessness with which they do it. But then you can't say that because as soon as you are thinking of saying it you notice that the girls – they all wear pigtails – are extremely pretty; so you are wooed away from such a treacherous thought and you decide that it is a very wonderful thing to devote your life, every day of it, to the odd business of spinning plates on sticks or standing on your hands with your feet keeping in continuous motion ten or more porcelain bowls. Then you find that one of the girls is in fact an elected deputy to the People's Congress, so presumably she spends some time there and can't give up *all* her hours to keeping porcelain bowls in the air with her feet. It is all very astonishing and I don't understand anything about it except what I've seen; but I would go almost any distance to see performers perform these curious things that do absolutely nothing to advance the state of the world or change human nature or help sick people.'

I wasn't so sure about that, and said so. 'If entertainment isn't important to people's lives . . .' – but clearly that would have led into philosophical depths that I had neither the equipment nor the wish to plumb. He nodded as if in agreement and we spoke of the vicarious nature of the thrills or wonderment experienced. 'After all, we are all human beings and it is just within the bounds of possibility – and I mean *just* – that each of us, given the time and the application and the early start, could walk the high wire or fill an empty stage with flowing fountains or the flags of all nations, or lugubriously tumble about a circus ring in grotesque disguise, or walk on nine-foot stilts, or lasso any specified leg of a galloping horse, or carry a man across Niagara Falls on a tightrope and pause in the middle to cook and eat an omelette, or escape from iron-bound boxes flung into the ocean, or achieve a multiplicity of leaps on and off a running horse, or dizzy the apprehensions of the audience by balancing upside down on a fingertip poised on a small globe that is in turn balanced on a stick . . .' We can airily say that there but for the idiosyncrasies of life . . . 'The thing is,' my companion said, 'the thing is that we can *identify*, not only with the miraculous achievement of it all but also with the *risk*, the *challenge*, the fear' (much of his conversation was in

SOME SKETCHES AT AN AQUARIUM SIDE-SHOW.

PROFESSOR STUART is the gentleman's name—another Professor—and flea-training is his profession. He occupies a dainty little theatre of red and white calico at the Royal Aquarium. On the board without is pasted a bill on which the tricks of the fleas are illustrated. It is not at all curious that the Professor's patrons move in the higher circles of society, at any rate it is a fact. The plebs say they have lots of them at home,

THE DUEL.

and pass along to less familiar attractions. The higher circles say they never saw one before, and cry "How curious!" This curiosity is probably what Mr. William Sloggins (now languishing in Pentonville) called "a bloomin' fairy tale," referring to the statement of his wife that the "kids was starvin'," and that it was a shame to give the beef-steak

"Why a shoeblack, Professor?" "Shoeblacks are always open to an honest job. I can't tell you why. I suppose"—very pensively—"because they're always brushing dirt away, and it exercises a healthy moral influence upon them."

ON THE TIGHT ROPE.

"But still, Professor they use a good deal of blacking in the practice of their profession." "Well, it's no use arguing, Mister. It's as I say. Shoeblacks

"ALL IN TO BEGIN."

HER MAJESTY'S MAILS.

to the dog. But "curious" is the expression all these bloods use. Sir William Harcourt dropped in to see the fleas one day, and watched the active little things go through their manœuvres with suppressed gusto. He did not say he had never seen one before, but at every jump a smile suffused his countenance, and he said, "Curious, very curious." Then, as he was walking away, he was heard to mutter, "Ah! me. What a lesson in jumping!" Now as to these manœuvres, which so pleased Sir William. These fleas—the troupe comprises about fifteen, like a football team (they are all chained, ladies, so squirm not)—are highly intelligent members of the *Pulex* family, who fire guns, draw hansoms, walk tight ropes, and perform other evolutions without a murmur. "This particular flea," said the Professor, "comes from a lodging-house at Bright—" I stopped the Professor, and said I was a pressman, and knew better.

are above suspicion, and when I give them a shilling I get my money's worth of the article required in return." "And where may the shoeblacks go to?" "They have their happy hunting grounds—and that's enough. I am of a secretive nature. Excuse me, but I see some—yes?"—and here the Professor put out his finger and his thumb, and approached my coat with the eager subtlety of a Sitting Bull on the war path. He then applied the magnifying glass, and with

THE FOUR-IN-HAND.

a look of disgust exclaimed, "It's not one of my sort. It's from a dog." "How curious!" I retorted, echoing Sir William. Having been relieved of my burden, I asked the Professor why not a doggy flea. "Because they are too wild; and they sigh so for their old home that they languish and die." "Of a broken heart, I suppose?" The Professor sighed, and began to tell me how he trained his little pets. "The great difficulty," he went on, "is to prevent their jumping. The first thing I do is to yoke them with this tiny chain of drawn wire, and then give them their own sweet way. They

"BEWARE OF THE DOG."

"Brighton," I said, "is much too voguish to hatch fleas." "Well, to tell you the truth," returned the flea-trainer, seeing that I would stand no gammon about Brighton—Margate would have been a different thing altogether—"when I ant a flea I give a shoeblack a shilling and he brings me a bottleful."

THE SWING BOAT.

soon tire, and then I attach them to their own particular vehicle. We begin business at about one in the afternoon. They are all in and ready

The Flea-Circus.

italics) 'which is why we experience — ' He fumbled somewhat ineffectually in his word-box for a moment. 'Excitement?' I suggested. 'Exactly,' he said. 'Excitement.'

Excitement: with which, of course, is bonded fear – fear that the performer might unbalance, or miss his hold, or suddenly become dizzy. And the fear is for our own performer-identified lives. He is too busy concentrating on his foothold or his judgement in the matter of distance; but we feel the hair rising in consequence of our inability to grasp the principles involved in flying through the air with the greatest of ease or in balancing, as Paul Cinquevalli did, large numbers of billiard balls on the tips of billiard cues. The breath is held, the suspension of belief is cancelled by the evidence of our eyes, we are witnesses of the impossible and are curiously warmed by the knowledge that we belong to the same race as those who perform the impossible. It is a quite different satisfaction from that arising from consideration of, for example, immense bravery: we automatically reject the idea that we could destroy a machine-gun post singlehanded or fly to virtually certain death in a bomb attack on an enemy dam, though we are still proud to belong to the same race as those who, without equivocation or fuss, do such things. We know we haven't the courage, physical or moral; but in the circus the searchlight of our observation is directed on what is clearly astonishing skill, and that it is also something else – courage, endurance, whatever – remains only a shadowy (if faintly uncomfortable) realization.

For aerialists and acrobats it is a far from shadowy realization. Death or injury are in constant, if distant, attendance. For the most dangerous tricks there may sometimes be the reassurance of a safety harness (called a 'mechanic' in the trade) or a net (Léotard used a spread of mattresses though he never plopped on to them). But the feeling, not unnaturally, is that audiences are better satisfied if there are no visible precautions. In 1908 at the Nouveau Cirque in Paris a team called the Fredianis mounted themselves into a three-high column on a trotting horse – the only time this feat has ever been achieved without the precaution of a mechanic – and eighteen people fainted with excitement or performer-identified fear. It is not uncommon for members of the audience to faint. Karl Wallenda, the senior member of the German high-wire family The Great Wallendas, recalled that in

An historic moment. The handbill
advertising Blondin's first
appearance in England.

Detroit in 1962 'they passed out in droves'. Making allowances for idiomatic exaggeration it isn't surprising that they did. The team had just completed a three-layer, seven-man pyramid on the wire when something went wrong – 'No one can tell what, a misjudgement by a hair's breadth, it is impossible to say' – and the pyramid collapsed, with the result that two of the team fell to their death and another (Karl's son) has been confined to a wheelchair ever since. 'The screams of the audience were hard to bear, and almost there was a panic, but not quite.' At seventy-one, a slender, thick-haired man who lives in the United States and still earns \$150,000 a year from high-wire walking, Karl came over to London in 1976 to act as a judge in the Circus World Championships which were held on Clapham Common. While here, he had a wire stretched between two wings of the Tower Hotel, Tower Bridge, at seventh-floor level and walked across, pausing to do a handstand in the middle – 'just for fun, I gained no money. It seems like a day wasted when there is no wire-walk; I have been doing it since I was a baby – so long that I don't remember when I started.'

The Circus World Championships that Karl Wallenda had come over to help judge are the brainchild of Prince Rainier of Monaco – who, like others I have mentioned, is whimsically able to have circuses come to him and perform more or less on his front lawn, since his entire principality covers rather less than a square mile and wherever a Big Top was erected it would be in view. Also, the Prince's family name is Grimaldi (Grimaldis have ruled Monaco since A.D. 968 except for a brief spell from 1815 to 1861, when somehow the King of Sardinia got into the act) and there can be no happier augury for the presence of a circus than that linkage in name with the most famous of clowns. (There could even be a family connexion; but in Genoa, where the family originated, and indeed throughout Italy, Grimaldis are as numerous as leaves on Vallombrosa, some high, some low in caste. The hardest done by of them was William, a Civil Servant in the War Office who in 1828, believing himself to be entitled to the hereditary title of marquis, went in search of the evidence, found it, and in sinking to his knees on his prie-dieu to thank God for His favours was seized by a fit of apoplexy and died before he could get the words out. You've got to be quick to get in before God does.) It was Prince Rainier's idea to hold annual Circus World Championships,

Weight-lifting; an old-time
strong-man's feat.

when stars of the calibre of Karl Wallenda have a look at the entrants and
see who is worthiest of the traditions of the Big Top. A good time is said to be
had by all, and contestants who may have in them the blood of bitter rivalries
from the days when they were trying to beat each other to the next venue,
merrily mingle, lend each other elephants to help push in the guy-rope pegs, and
wish each other luck. As time draws toward the judging of each individual circus
(the championships are spread over five days) equestriennes and animal trainers
and jugglers and clowns and veterinarians and acrobats appear about the Big Top
in curious motley of spangles and parkas, mackintoshes and wellington boots,
putting their hands to this, that and the other (circus people are nothing if not a
co-operative body) as, inevitably, the rain falls and an anticipatory apprehension
falls with it. This time, they know, the only members of the audience they have
to perform for are the judges, and the judges have a knowing eye for the finer
points as well as for the total impact made on the invited audience. Nobody's eye
could be more knowing, or for that matter steadier, than Karl Wallenda's –
'Though it is best not to let it consider the ground too much,' he says instructively.
And since he holds the world's record for the highest high-wire act his hint is not
to be ignored. On 18 July 1970, when he was sixty-five, he walked across the
Tallulah Gorge, Georgia, U.S.A., with 750 feet of emptiness below him. He took
just over a quarter of an hour to make the journey of 233 yards, including a
couple of pauses to stand on his head. 'The height is immaterial,' he says, sounding
remarkably like Lady Bracknell. 'Ask any steeplejack or workman engaged in
the construction of high buildings.' There weren't any steeplejacks around to ask,
but I wouldn't have bothered anyway. If Karl Wallenda said so I'm sure it's
right. I'll keep my acrophobia to myself. Blondin, when he crossed Niagara, had
only 160 feet between him and the Falls, and when some winsome girl asked him
whether the very word 'Falls' didn't inspire him with terror he answered stonily,
'No, Madame; there is no terror in a word.' But the difference between 750 feet
and 160 feet is neither here nor there if you're falling through them. (By the way,
the fidgety man he carried pick-a-back across Niagara and threatened to dump in
the middle if he didn't stop fidgeting, was his agent – a man named Harry
Colcord. Many artistes in the field of entertainment have seen sinister motives in

Skills on the tight-rope;
beating the drum, from
an eighteenth-century
French engraving.

the enterprise.) And what if you're asleep? The most extraordinary – as distinct from daring, though, God knows, there was plenty of daring involved too – high-wire act was that of Henri Rochetain, who, in 1973, when he was forty-seven, *lived* on a tightrope 400 feet long, stretched between two towers 82 feet above the French town of Saint Etienne, for six months. Nobody, including himself, can understand how he slept without falling off. But there he was, poised over the coal mines and armaments factories, literally alone and palely loitering, trotting up and down the wire every now and again to give himself some exercise and covering a total of 310 miles in the process. His only reward for this astonishing feat of endurance seems to have been a few thousand francs and a lifetime retainer from the firm that made his shoes. He did better the year before, when he made the longest recorded high-wire walk in the history of funambulism – just over two miles, which he accomplished in three and a third hours – and, according to *Paris-Soir* was the richer by a million francs. And not a franc too much, if you ask me.

What people *have* asked me, most of the time I've been collecting material for this book, and most eagerly, is about the animals. Circuses and menageries are bound up with each other for reasons I hope I've made clear – the main one being, as was established in the days of the Roman emperors, that people are curious and can always be enticed to see creatures that are to them strange, or indigenous creatures that have been trained to do remarkable things, or both; and that men with a streak of the entrepreneur in them have gone to some trouble to satisfy this curiosity and at the same time line their own pockets. They have also, in a sense, advanced human knowledge, since there have been those in the field of natural history and zoology whose deductions from the study of animals have led to advantageous things. John Hunter, for example, whose dissecting of exotic animals in his dissecting room at Earls Court has already been mentioned, enlarged the bounds of anatomical research more than any other medical man in a lifetime; while the search for rare beasts has led to the discovery and opening up of new horizons – not necessarily for the good of mankind, but that's another story.

My own appreciation of performing animals is not enthusiastic. With the possible exception of horses, whose attitude since the earliest days of their domestication

Skills on the tight-rope;
playing the violin, from
an eighteenth-century
French engraving.

has been a more or less total co-operation (possibly because they haven't the independence of spirit natural to wilder creatures), I am not pleased by their antics. I do not find it funny to see an elephant wearing a tiny hat or sitting on a tiny stool; I am not amused by chimpanzees in ridiculous clothing demonstrating their agility in a series of routines imposed on them by their trainers; I am not thrilled by human heads inside lions' mouths. On the other hand, I am not one of those who believe that the training of animals to perform unnatural tricks can be accomplished only by cruelty or inspiring fear. It is clear to me that such can be achieved only by patience and understanding of the character of the particular animal, just as one can train a dog to round up sheep or retrieve a bird, or lead a blind person about, or distinguish between a criminal and a goodie, only by a system of patience and reward and endless repetition. But whether accomplished by patience and understanding or not, I cannot see that creatures that have no choice in the matter and whose natural habits and habitats are not domestic should have imposed on them a chummy domesticity that robs them of dignity – and, incidentally, in the theft thereof robs the trainer of some of his too. But he, like those who elect to stand on their heads on a three-inch rope with nothing but a 750-foot chasm below them, has a choice in the matter. There lies the difference, and I shall say no more about it except to add that I put the activity of wild beast training fairly low down in the scale of necessary functions of the human race, which I think could well survive without it.

Circuses, on the other hand, probably couldn't. They don't always survive even with it. In 1976 Circus Britannia, owned and run by an ex-Chipperfields man, Count (well, I mentioned the love of circus buffs for titles) Maximilian Lazard, went under the auctioneer's hammer, despite the fact that it had a Himalayan bear called Yogi that could waltz, roll barrels, and kiss its trainer; three lions; two pumas; a black leopard; and a lot of performing dogs. The cost of renting a site to put the Big Top on – £100 a day – plus the cost of travel and feeding the animals – £1 a day for a bear, the same for a lion – had forced it to fold its tent and steal away. The Count once asked the Pope to give the circus its blessing, which he did. It made Britannia unique, but it didn't improve the economical situation. So, performing animals regardless, this particular Greatest Show on Earth didn't

Its eager course *Mazeppa's* horse
No longer runs with wild career;
And MISTER HICKS no longer sticks
To bare-back'd steed 'mid shout and cheer.

That aged man, the weeping *Khan*,
Has ceas'd to hug his long lost son;
The *Tyrant Greek* his pound a week
Has lost—his occupation gone !

A lament on the substitution of
'The Scenes in the Circle' for
'The Historic Drama' at Astley's;
drawings by Tenniel from
Punch, 1851.

survive. 'On the other hand,' the Count is reported as saying, 'two new ones set out last year, and that must have meant at least twenty-five thousand pounds for the establishment of each of them. You don't get an Arts Council grant, you know – though personally I think there's a good case for giving one, because a circus is just as much the people's entertainment as ballet is, or opera, or the theatre. But there you are – you don't get it and that's all about it. So you rely on box-office takings and if you don't get up to three hundred pounds a day you're sunk, because you've nothing in hand at the end of the season to see you through the winter. The big circuses are all right because they're usually public companies that people have invested in; and I had a hope that Tesco or some other big group might have been alive to the possibilities of sponsoring us, but it didn't happen. All the same, even without our little lot' – a gesture embracing the dismantled rows of seats – 'there are fifteen circuses on the road today in Britain alone, so nobody can say the business is dead.'

Nobody thought of saying it anyway. At the time of this writing preparations are being made for the Silver Jubilee of Queen Elizabeth, and the B.B.C. are going to televise a circus-and-variety show that will be held in what the papers call the Biggest Big Top In The World. It'll have to be pretty big to merit the title. There's one in Las Vegas called Circus Circus that covers an area of 129,000 square feet with the actual top of the Big Top ninety feet above the ground; and there's another in Moscow into which you can stuff 3,200 people. But size isn't the really important thing, despite all the superlatives that are scattered around fairs and Big Top sites. Batty's, the nineteenth-century circus that Grace Darling was tricked into appearing in as a sensation after her rescue of nine people from the wrecked *Forfarshire* in 1838, had only two 'learned' horses (which could write in the sawdust, distinguish between different-coloured handkerchiefs, and count), six performing dogs, a clown, a ringmaster – Mr Batty himself, who doubled as the animal trainer and keeper of the box-office – and a stilt walker who, unstilted, was also an acrobat; Bertram Mills Circus had, in its 1948 run at Olympia, London, forty-eight different acts. But they were both, to proprietors and public alike, The Greatest Show on Earth.

More circus characters by
Tenniel, from *Punch*, 1851.

Glossary

ANTIPODIST A juggler – but one who stands on his head or lies in a trinka and juggles with his feet.

AUGUSTE The fall guy or feed in a duo of clowns; the one that gets slapped; the butt of all the tricks.

BALLOONS Hoops through which acrobats and acrobatic animals jump; sometimes flaming, sometimes with paper stretched across them. Hoops juggled with by jugglers are called rings.

BEARER The ground partner in an act in which the bearer balances a long pole on his head while his partner shins up it and performs tricks while perched aloft (Perch Act).

BENDER In short, a contortionist. But the word is inadequate to describe the astonishing things he does with his body and limbs – such as combing his hair with a comb held in the toes of one foot while with the other foot he scratches an armpit.

CATCHER The one who catches the partner (voltiger) in any flying trapeze or aerial acrobatic act.

FUNAMBULIST A rope- or wire-walker. (From Latin *funis*, rope; *ambulare*, to walk.)

JOEY A clown. So called after Joseph Grimaldi.

JOSSER You and me; anyone not in the circus or show business.

LIBERTIES Not, as one might think, unwelcome advances made to coy ladies. Liberty horses are those magnificent animals (often Arabs) you see plumed and

The Scots Greys and Napoleon,
by Tenniel.

caparisoned, who perform beautiful evolutions and remarkable tricks without any physical contact with their trainer.

LOT, THE The ground on which the Big Top is pitched.

MECHANIC (or LUNGE) A safety harness attached to a wire, used by aerial artistes in tricks of potentially extreme danger, or for practising.

MIDDLEMAN (-MEN) The second and/or third storey in any human pyramidal construction.

PERCH ACT See BEARER.

RUN-IN CLOWN The circus equivalent to the theatre's front-cloth act. The run-in clown (who may or may not be a star in his own right, for circus people are immensely co-operative) has the job of keeping the crowd amused while preparations are made for the next act.

SOMERSAULT Well, we all know what a somersault is; but in the circus it can take a variety of forms – backward, forward, on the ground or in mid-air, on and off horses, and in single, double, triple, and quadruple measures.

STAR-BACKS The posh seats. Better upholstered than the others, and naturally more expensive.

TOP-MOUNTER The top storey, the summit, of any human pyramidal construction.

TRINKA A cradle for an antipodist to lie in while he juggles with his feet.

UNDERSTANDER(S) The base storey in any human pyramidal construction.

VOLTIGE(R) In equestrian acts the act of vaulting on to or off a horse; in aerial acts the voltiger is the partner who flies through the air with the greatest of ease to be caught by the catcher.

A fine pencil drawing of an
elephant by Allers, 1887.

Bibliography

BARNUM, P. T. *Struggles and Triumphs*. Buffalo, 1889.

BOSTOCK, E. H. *Menageries, Circuses and Theatres*. London, 1927.

DISHER, M. WILLSON. *Clowns and Pantomimes*. London, 1925
    The Greatest Show on Earth. London, 1937.

EIPPER, PAUL. *Circus*. London, 1931.

HENDERSON, J. Y. *Circus Doctor*. London, 1952.

LLOYD, JAMES. *My Circus Life*. London, 1925.

LUKENS, JOHN. *The Sanger Story*. London, 1925.

MACGREGOR-MORRIS, PAMELA. *Chipperfield's Circus*. London, 1957.

SANGER, 'LORD' GEORGE. *Seventy Years a Showman*. London, 1926.

SMITH, LADY ELEANOR. *British Circus Life*. London, 1948.
    Life's a Circus. London, 1939.

TYRWHITT-DRAKE, SIR GARRARD. *The English Circus and Fairground*. London, 1946.

WERNER, M. R. *Barnum*. New York, 1923.

The above were the principal sources consulted. Those wishing to embark upon a lifetime's reading and studying of the subject can do no better than to begin with: STOTT, RAYMOND TOOLE. *Circus and Allied Arts*. London, 1958-62, the three volumes of which are a monument to circus bibliography. But back to the lesser

Acrobatic and musical animals,
trained by travelling performers, in
the thirteenth century.

shores of scholarship! I also found the following books useful in writing the present study:

BALSDON, J. P. V. D. *Life and Leisure in Ancient Rome*. London, 1969.

CHESNEY, KELLOW. *The Victorian Underworld*. London, 1970.

GRAVES, CHARLES. *Mr Punch's History of Modern England*. London, 1921.

HART, ROGER. *English Life in Chaucer's Day*. London, 1973.
English Life in Tudor Times. London, 1972.
English Life in the Eighteenth Century. London, 1970.

MUMFORD, LEWIS. *The City in History*. London, 1961.

SCOTT, A. F. *Every One a Witness: The Norman Age*. London, 1976.
Every One a Witness: The Plantagenet Age. London, 1975.
Every One a Witness: The Tudor Age. London, 1975.
Every One a Witness: The Stuart Age. London, 1974.

Acknowledgements

The quotation from *Clowns and Pantomimes* by M. Willson Disher is reproduced by courtesy of the publishers, CONSTABLE & CO., LTD. The illustrations on pages 10, 16, 22, 24, 30, 36, 38, 42, 44, 48, 54, 56, 60, 82, 96, 98, 100, 102, 104, 106, and 124 are reproduced with the permission of the RADIO TIMES – HULTON PICTURE LIBRARY.

A NOTE ON THE TYPEFACE

This book was composed on the Monotype in Bembo, Series 270, a face originally cut by Francesco Griffo for the great Venetian printer Aldus Manutius who first used it for a short Latin tract, de Aetna, written by Cardinal Bembo and published in 1495. It is the earliest and undoubtedly the most beautiful of all old face designs in the history of typography and its profound influence throughout Europe over the succeeding centuries cannot be over-emphasised. It was copied by Claude Garamond in Paris, and by Robert Granjon for Christophe Plantin and others. It took deep root in the Low Countries and was re-cut by van Dijck; and it was this version that William Caslon took as his model when the English typefounding trade was revived in the 18th century. The italic for Bembo was based on a chancery face of the great writing-master Giovanni Tagliente (1524) and is a perfect match for the roman. The re-cutting undertaken by the Monotype Corporation dates from 1929.